C000050498

LEON
& MONIQUE

L. Hughes

Copyright © L. Hughes 2021
This book is sold subject to the condition that it shall not, by way of trade or
otherwise, be lent, resold, hired out, or otherwise circulated without the
publisher's prior consent in any form of binding or cover other than that in which
it is published and without a similar condition including this condition being
imposed on the subsequent publisher.
The moral right of L. Hughes has been asserted.
ISBN-13: 9798758264805

This is a work of fiction. Names, characters, businesses, organisations, places, events and incidents either are the product of the author's imagination or are used fictitiously. Any resemblance to actual persons, living or dead, events, or locales is entirely coincidental.

I dedicate this book to the teachings of Rhonda Byrne.

CONTENTS

Chapter 1

She closed her eyes. This did not help. Dizzy, more than before.

When she opened them again, he was standing. Raising her fear once more.

"Get back I said. Don't come any closer." Scrambling to get to her feet.

She was a step from the edge of the end of her life. It was something she could not see.

He froze on the spot. Four paces away. Shaking all over with dread.

If she moved a fraction it would all be over, and she would surely be dead.

It was a warm summer evening and little did he know.

The love of his life was about to show.

He sat, sipping juice, outside a beach-house plot.

Thinking of nothing in this heavenly spot.

The sea was real quiet. A perfect sound to the ear.

He was very thankful life had brought him here.

A scent, on the air, drifted into his nose.

Perfume so sweet. It must be worn by a rose.

He breathed it again. It was just, so nice.
His feelings switched on, now he had enjoyed it twice.
A long, slender shadow appeared on the sand.
What beauty owns this that graces the land?
He took off his sunglasses and raised his eyes.
Her perfume, now stronger, brought his soul alive.
As soon as he saw her, he knew right at that time.
His heart fell in love. Thoughts of, *Would she be mine?*
She looked at him and gave an acknowledging smile.
He was completely awe-struck for the very first time.
He said, "Hello. How are you feeling today?"
It seemed the most sensible thing he could say.
She said, "I'm very well and, how are you?"
He was spinning with excitement. He sensed she knew.
She had beautiful, peaceful, drawing eyes.
Her gentle voice had him mesmerised.
Her skin was smooth. The sun made it look nice.
He said, "Would you like to join me, for a juice with ice?"
She looked so perfect in her light, cotton dress.
The expression on her face was so free from stress.
She had a calming presence that shone right through.
He prayed she'd say yes and take up a pew.
"I'd like that," she replied. He was floating on air.
He stood and moved round to offer her a chair.
Like a princess, as she sat, taking everything in.
Her hair drifting lightly on the warm sea wind.
He thought, *Is this really happening, right now, to me?*
Expecting to wake up from a wonderful dream.
He went into the house to make her a drink.
Completely shaking. He could barely think.
Returning, a lot calmer, he set her drink down.

Her smile stole his heart as she turned around.
"Thank you," she said. "You're welcome," he replied.
For him, these exchanges were electrified.
He asked her name. She had him filled with mystique.
She glanced at the sky and whispered, "Monique."
He said, "What a beautiful name. It so suits you.
She is called Monique. Here to take in the view."
She laughed, rather pleased, at his rhyming statement.
Then said, "Maybe we could make a more formal
arrangement."
On hearing her words, he nearly fell off his chair.
A date with this angel simply could not compare.
She was just so pretty and shaped to perfection.
Those gorgeous, blue eyes enriched her complexion.
"Then let me take you to dinner. The honour would be
mine."
His voice slightly nervous with his bold, bare-faced line.
She said, "Yes, you can. To a nice place with a view.
By the way, what do I call you?"
He said, "My name is Leon. That's who I am.
How does that sound, to you, sweet madame?"
"I like it." She smiled. "What is going on?
The two names float together. Monique and Leon."
As he heard her words a calm silence fell.
It fell on him and what it did I will tell.
He was tumbling in circles. His blood instantly warm.
Fingertips tingling and so much more.
Breaths became quick. His heart beat like a drum.
Then a doorway opened as his being turned numb.
His soul was lifted through a cloud, so white.
It blinded his eyes and removed his sight.

Then he stopped…He just lay. He'd never felt so full.
He had the feeling of being wrapped in cotton wool.
He was swimming on his back with apparent ease.
Splashing around in the hand of loves' seas.
He could hear her sweet voice repeating his name.
He shook back to his body and back in his brain.
She had her hand on his shoulder. Giving him a shake.
He looked left and right to check he was awake.
"What happened there?" she asked, rather flat.
"Forgive me," he said. "I have tendency to do that."
"To do what?" was her question. How would he explain?
He decided to tell her to see if her feelings would change.
"Well, sometimes I hear things. They take me away.
To that part of my mind where the child likes to play.
Where I dream my best dreams and answers are provided.
The sun always shines, and I am never undecided.
I know it exists in my heart and mind.
When I go there, I go and completely unwind.
Tiredness and time leave me alone for a while.
With one look on my face. That being, a smile.
So much is given when I slip to that place.
I wish I could share its glorious pace.
I imagine being able to take someone with me.
To the place that's so right, so warm and so cheery.
I really do float and get totally lost.
The beautiful thing is that it comes with no cost.
It all just makes sense. It fits right in my life.
Then when I return, I am free from all strife.
I meet certain people. They help send me there.
With a look that they give or words that they share."
He turned round and looked at her, somewhat, enquiring.

Two thin streaks of tears. She was smiling and crying.
"Was it something I said? Do you think it absurd?"
"No. That is the most beautiful thing I've ever heard."
They were joyful tears. He felt so good.
He knew, in his heart, that she understood.
Unable to withhold or withstand the sheer bliss.
He cupped her face in his hands to offer a first kiss.
She closed her eyes. Her mouth opened slightly.
As she moistened her lips ever so lightly.
She became a little dazed. Her feelings were high.
Dancing through air like a free butterfly.
She felt so much going on in that short space of time.
Her senses revolving and spiralling high.
She felt herself slipping and sliding in love.
With no reason to resist or the need of a shove.
She felt his warm breath. She angled her head.
All that she was now hung on a thread.
Flooded with feelings in a world with no pain.
So many thoughts speeding through her brain.
Then one little kiss given, almost to tease.
And that succumbing feeling one gets in their knees.
Her sound, breathing in, made him kiss her once more.
A moment of love for them both to adore.
They both shook at the same time from the long, second kiss.
Looking at each other like they'd been granted a wish.
He said, "Can I be honest and outright from the very start?
The moment I saw you, something changed in my heart."
She said, "It's funny you should say that because when I saw you.
I knew there and then, what I felt was true."
They stood up together, almost cheek-to-cheek.

Realising then, there was no need to speak.
He cradled her sleek body close to his own.
She placed her hands on his nape and released a slight groan.
Their lips met again. They let love lead the way.
A perfect vision one could craft out of clay.
They held onto each other wanting never to let go.
No beginning or end, just a reciprocal flow.
It was all so easy that they smiled through the kisses.
Like a reunion with someone your heart truly misses.
A level had been found, they had not been to before.
This intensified their passion, so it grew all the more.
Then they stopped, for a time, to look at the other.
Knowing they would make the perfect lover.
It was moving so fast but what did they care?
They knew what they felt. They were very much aware.
All else was forgotten at the edge of the brine.
This was their single-most, life-changing time.
There could not have been a better place or location,
For two people to feel this most powerful sensation.
The moon had appeared as a rest for the sun.
Giving light to the sand where something wonderful had
begun.
Monique looked at Leon. He smiled at her eyes.
Then she turned her face to the star-filled skies.
He wanted to speak but he was barely able.
His heart was touched as if seeing an angel.
The moon's white light seemed to make her face shine.
A picture, in his mind, he could hold for all time.
She knew he was looking. Her eyes flicked to his.
"Leon," she said. "I want more than a kiss."
They let go their embrace and took a slow walk.

Heightened excitement as they passed through the door.

Holding each other's hand as they moved to the bedroom.

Feelings came together as if drawn to a vacuum.

She stood in front with her back facing him.

Looked over her shoulder with a warming grin.

He'd noticed earlier, a thought he could not impress.

She was completely naked under her white, cotton dress.

The sash window, half-open, passed air through the shade.

A breeze on thin curtains as they moved like waves.

He reached for her top button. His fingers a little shaken.

Knowing, in his mind, his feelings were now taken.

He undone the last and took a long, deep breath.

Reached for her shoulders to remove her dress.

Just as his hands were to touch her gown.

Her smile was gone. There replaced by a frown.

She slipped from his touch and glided round the bed.

He could only smile as his face turned red.

There was an unlit candle, in a bottle, on a stool.

To bring romantic light to the darkening room.

She leaned forward and picked up a single match.

From her body her dress did slowly detach.

It fell to her elbows as she struck up a flame.

Her bare flesh, exposed, belonged in a frame.

She stood straight up and turned around.

Allowing her dress to fall to the ground.

She beautifully shone with pure female delight.

A swaying ambience against the flickering light.

She began moving her palms slowly over her skin.

He could only feel love for what his eyes took in.

She ran down her thighs, then caressed at her hips.

Her eyes were shut as she pursed her lips.

He could not interrupt her whilst she felt this desire.
Her heart was thumping. She climbed higher and higher.
He longed to go to her. He removed his clothing.
Her breaths became louder. Her body was glowing.
"Oh yes!" she said as she opened her eyes.
Expecting him clothed. She was pleasantly surprised.
"Come to me, my love. Hold me tight to you.
I want to feel close like grass and dew.
Lay with me between these soft covers.
And let us release our truest colours.
I have never felt a feeling so high.
It's like I could fly and touch the sky.
I'm already in love. It's right there in you.
This must surely be a dream come true.
Touch me, so I know you are here.
Let go of all your passion and have no fear."
He moved towards her and placed a hand on her head.
Turned her round gently and lay her on the bed.
They could not hold back as the moment moved on.
Monique grabbed him tight and said, "I love you Leon."
"And I love you, beautiful Monique.
I could not be more honest with the words I speak.
Your lips, your eyes, your body and your face.
The sound when you talk. Your perfect ways.
The look you give. How you hold yourself.
The peace in your smile. Your fragrance as well.
How you show me your feelings. I just have to look.
Like turning the pages of my favourite book.
No effort, at all, to be here with you.
No effort, at all, to fall in love too."
Her soul was drifting almost on the air.

Never, in her life, was she so free of care.
The most marvellous sensation from the words that were
spoken.
Pleasure exuded through her every emotion.
Even in the midst of this most loving scene.
She could smile and laugh, sing or scream.
"Oh, how lucky I feel at this very time.
Knowing, Leon, that you will be mine.
You have filled my soul. Your words are so kind.
You thread them together to float in my mind.
It's like dancing naked, at midnight, on the sand.
And having you there to hold my hand.
I hear the wind. I can smell the sea.
Not a soul in sight. Only you and me.
Make love to me now, that I may feel your fire.
Speak in my ear with all your desire.
I could not be more ready, for you, right here.
Unleash all your passion on me, my dear."
They made love together. A beautiful scene.
Something you could only imagine was a dream.
They twisted and turned and rolled around.
The air was full of their loving sound.
Stroking of bodies. Soft skin was kissed.
The tenderest touch between their lips.
Her hair, soaked with sweat, lay on his chest.
Holding her close to let her rest.
He kissed her head. She let go a sigh.
She pulled the sheet up to cover her thigh.
The cool, evening air let its presence be known.
Two lovers had let their feelings be shown.
She tilted her head so they could look at each other.

One last little peek as he pulled up the cover.
"Monique that was the most passionate love I have made.
You brought something from me which lay in the shade.
I have never been made to feel so alive.
Feelings within that already thrive.
I must be with you for more than this night.
To be in your presence is sheer delight."
"It will be so, for I also feel blessed.
Lying here, with you close to my chest.
I dream of tomorrow and opening my eyes.
You looking at me as you lie at my side.
It's the fullest feeling I cannot keep in.
With a gentle voice I could peacefully sing."
The candle burnt out. Not a moment too soon.
A shroud of darkness filled the room.
In each other's arms, there beneath the sheet.
A few seconds passed as they both fell asleep.
The first, easing, sound of the tide rolling in.
Opened their eyes, for their day to begin.
A long, loving kiss whilst their eyes closed once more.
Thoughts of last night brought feelings to the fore.
He pressed himself on her. She accepted with no attempt.
The rest of existence became completely spent.
Two friends, poles apart, who never knew.
Love at first sight had, surely, come true.
His arms wrapped around her as though she were a part of him.
Timelessness bound them like tonic and gin.
Like the most exotic tango that needs no correction.
Or a waltz that breathes complete perfection.
With every thrust, their bodies jolted with elation.

Totally immersed in a combined revelation.
The salt in the air joined their sexual release,
As they were fired high into a transcending peace.
She moved with grace like love itself.
Domineering manoeuvres and such divine stealth.
Like slow air rolling beneath a sheet of silk.
It could not be matched by any comparative ilk.
There was a special feeling, making love on this morning.
A brilliant beginning. A brand-new dawning.
Her knees reached out wide. She made sounds of pleasure.
Like opening a chest and discovering lost treasure.
With her head on the pillow, she looked out at the ocean.
Connected, in-love, as though they shared the same motion.
This was all of pure love sharing its power.
Cascading and growing with every passing hour.
They knew in their hearts this could last forever.
Now, to make the most of a lifetime together.

Chapter 2

The cold, first few seconds burst from the shower.
Leon's face in his hands. His mind on his flower.
The water warmed up and heated his skin.
He now believed what had happened to him.
She was in his feelings and in his head.
He pictured her, naked, lying in the bed.
Monique was perfect in every way.
A ray of sunshine for each new day.
He closed his eyes and put his face to the spray.
Not wanting to wash her scent away.
A sigh of joy. A feeling so right.
Made him smile with pure delight.
His mind started wandering through the love they had made.
Picking out moments that each of them played.
He reached for the soap and was about to wash,
When she wrapped her arms round him and gave him a shock.
He felt her chin rest on his shoulder.
Then he turned around so he could hold her.
She took the soap and worked up lather.
Then said, "I'll do that, for you, if you'd rather."
Her soapy hands slid and moved all around.

He stood and looked down as she knelt to the ground.
She stared back at him with loving eyes,
As she moved her hands up and down his thighs.
Here and there, she scraped at his skin.
Her face could not have been closer to him.
Then she bent right down and kissed his feet.
It was like a beautiful painting from ancient Greece.
She stood up and took the shower from the wall.
Watered him down. Then stood up tall.
Handed him the soap. She was happy as could be.
"Now, my love, will you please bathe me?"
He rubbed her back with gentle sweeps.
Bubbles rolled down between her cheeks.
Her head moved loosely and fell back on his chest.
His hands came around to find her breasts.
She clasped her hands behind his head.
Soap ran down, between her legs.
Her knees shook fiercely and almost give in.
Spontaneous sex was about to begin.
He bit lightly and gently on the back of her neck.
With both her hands she held her breasts.
He turned the dial, so the water cooled down.
It took her breath and shook her to the ground.
She put her hands on the wall and spread her feet.
Needing that feeling of being complete.
Her body sparkled with every drop that fell.
She wanted it now and he could tell.
He pulled back her elbows. Her chest pushed out.
An assertive entry made her instantly shout.
It was wild. It was frantic. She almost stood on her toes.
From between her legs a mighty orgasm rose.

She broke free from his hands and gripped the cold pipe,
To embrace the most sexual explosion of her life.
With his hands on her hips, he took a firm hold.
He yelled from deep down with a feeling untold.
She screamed uncontrollably as she reached her peak.
Dizziness near swept her off her feet.
Then she leaned back to him. He was still deep inside.
They swayed together in a gentle ride.
She turned for a kiss while she still had the feeling.
Her slim body shook against his heavy breathing.
He threw both arms around her as their lips lightly met.
A glorious feeling they would never forget.
He reached for a towel as she turned the tap off.
And he wrapped her in it, like a jewel in a cloth.
She had not quite landed whilst he was drying her down.
Still shaking as her blood was pumping around.
She brought one hand to her face and covered her eyes.
Panting as he touched her, which she could not disguise.
"Are you OK Monique? Shall I stop, just for now?
Your legs are still quivering. Would you like to lie down?"
She was still having orgasms, in waves, uncontrolled.
Holding her head, her eyes opened and closed.
He put his arm round her back. Then picked up her legs.
She just fell to his hold and dropped back her head.
He moved toward the door to place her on the bed.
Her limp, naked body, in his arms, outspread.
Placing her down, he then lay at her side.
Stroking her body to help her revive.
"I've just been to a place I've never visited before.
Like I had left my body and went off to explore.
I could hear my screams and I heard you shout.

Then a wave swept through me like I was passing out.
The rush just kept coming. I thought it would never end.
My whole universe shook. I cannot pretend.
These last moments are a blur. I don't know how I got here.
I have just had my most powerful orgasm, my dear."
He said, "I'll make us some coffee and a bite to eat.
You just lie there and relax, my sweet.
Just put nice thoughts right into your head.
For today, I shall bring you your breakfast in bed."
He picked himself up and strolled out the room.
Into the kitchen to prepare some food.
She curled herself up into a nice, comfy ball.
Admiring a painting that hung on the wall.
A pencilled sketch of a naked female.
Sublimely accurate in every detail.
The body of a goddess with no discernible face.
She was totally covered in a thin sheet of lace.
Monique's eyes shifted to the left-hand corner.
Something there that instantly drawn her.
A small inscription she could barely see.
When she focused her eyes it simply said "She."
Lying back, she pondered its meaning for a while.
Then, in the end, all she could do was smile.
Leon entered, carrying a large tray with legs.
"Orange juice, coffee, toast and scrambled eggs?"
"Lovely!" she said. "But what about you?"
He laughed at her humour. "Oh, there's enough for two."
They sat, comfortably naked, eating and drinking.
The picture on the wall. Monique could not stop thinking.
"Leon, when I look at that picture I want to start dreaming.
Does it bear any significance or hold special meaning?"

"Well, Monique, I can tell you this.
The picture you see is one of pure bliss.
It is the essence of all women. Which means the world to me.
When I drew it, I could only call her 'She.'"
Surely the work of a professional was Monique's thought.
Leon's door had opened with this modest purport.
She enquired with zeal, "It must be something you adore.
A thought or a feeling you are able to draw.
And this image, so beautiful, that has come from you.
A rare gift indeed, only given to few.
Do you draw a lot? Can you show me some more?
I have seen no more pictures on any other wall."
He smiled at her passion. For her desire to delve in.
Then said, "I know just the place where we can begin.
I have a gallery where my best work is displayed.
At a town close to here in an exclusive arcade.
I am closed at the moment. The place needs some renewing.
But I will gladly give you a personal viewing.
I have sold many paintings. The last, to a famed actor.
The feedback I get is that my work is sought after.
We can take the train. There's a stop nearby.
Then it's just a short walk along the cobbled, canal side.
There's the nicest coffee shop placed right next door.
With seating outside, to enjoy the feel so much more.
It's relaxing and peaceful on nice, sunny days.
There's a cellist who busks and you drift as he plays.
Sounds bounce off the buildings with every note he picks.
As you sip on your coffee and feel the acoustics.
I hope you will like my other works.
It's a moment like this that stirs my nerves.
I'd love you to see them and feel what I've drawn.

Though, some you may like. Others you'll be torn.
I am a commissioned artist. It's what I love to do.
I could paint many beautiful pictures of you."
She was highly excited from all that he'd said.
He painted beautiful pictures, right there, in her head.
"Can we go right away? It sounds so appealing.
I feel like a child who's hardly believing.
An artist. That's nice. You suit your career.
I would love you to paint pictures of me, my dear.
I can see it now. Me posing for you.
Rolled out on a chaise-longue. I'd be naked too.
Music would play in my mind as you begin.
Whilst a fan on the ceiling was cooling my skin.
A touch of love with every stroke of your brush.
All the colours of the rainbow to make it so lush.
But unlike any other that sat whilst you paint.
This subject would love you without a single constraint.
You could paint love on your canvas from deep inside.
As I bare my body with nothing to hide.
I would struggle with desire to lie there so still.
As you peered, here and there, it would give me a thrill.
When you were done and placed your brush down.
I would cover myself in a black, satin gown.
You not wishing me to come over or even stand.
Would turn it to me with a stroke of your hand.
And there on the canvas, in fine detail, to see.
A picture of a rainbow that pours over me.
Drenching my skin with every colour that's known.
As I lay like a feather, on a long leather throne.
You perfectly catch every curve I possess.
A picture to dive into and passionately caress.

A masterpiece of your brilliance caught in one scene.
For a buyer to admire as if they were in a dream."
He could hardly respond to her heartfelt suggestion.
Did he start with an answer or even a question?
Then he spoke really soft after, what seemed, a long time.
"I've never had a thought so clearly plucked from my mind.
A chaise-longue and rainbows was my very first thought.
When I pictured painting you to hang on my wall.
You have totally intrigued me ever since our eyes met.
But this is a moment I will never forget."
They both got dressed and didn't say a word.
The sea and seagulls is all that was heard.
The town was all that he'd said and so much more.
Her eyes lit up as she opened the train door.
They arrived at the gallery. The shutter was raised.
There were also bars and it was heavily glazed.
"I see you have yourself a fortress to safeguard your art.
Let's go in and make a start."
All the paintings, on easels, were covered in white cloaks.
Standing upright and stout. Looking like ghosts.
"OK," he said. "Shall we remove these sheets?
See if what's behind them, in any way, speaks."
And as each painting was slowly uncovered,
Monique was astounded by what she discovered.
Then one painting stood out from all the material.
A magnificent image of something ethereal.
It was a man and a woman. They both had white wings.
She plays the harp as he watches and sings.
The place that they're in is not of this plane.
Leon noticed her gaze and went over to explain.
He approached from the side and could see she was touched.

Right at that moment he loved her so much.
She took it in and could see their love was undying.
A closer look revealed the woman to be crying.
"Leon, why does she cry in something so beautiful?"
"I will convey the meaning which may prove to be useful.
He is singing his last song for he is to leave forever.
He will move to his next life. They will no longer be together.
The words of the song are about what they've shared.
And how she is the one for who he has always cared.
He sings about leaving. How he must fly away.
He never wants to see the end of this day.
He is her one true love. She feels his pain.
She cries at knowing she'll never see him again.
She is so in love. She plays from her soul.
As she cries for love that she must let go.
What you are looking at is something I seen.
I painted this image because it appeared in a dream.
I draw inspiration from a wide range of themes.
People, love, desire and dreams.
Then I take time out to unclothe what I feel.
And transform that beauty into something real.
I try to see love when I paint or draw.
And the most beautiful images come to the fore.
I can only paint when I feel this way.
Every feeling I've had is here on display.
But the thing I love is when new feelings rise.
They burst from my body and cover the skies.
I know I can do anything because love is here.
Love can turn a simple man into a seer.
Love guides my feelings and makes them all true.
They flow from me now, standing next to you."

They smiled at each other. Their hearts did race,
As they came together in a loving embrace.
Their eyes were closed as they held on tight.
Breathed each other's scent and felt so right.
"So, tell me Monique, more about you.
A person so special. What is it you do?"
They stared at each other as she started to tell.
"I write tales of my adventures and I've done fairly well.
I document the facts and turn it into a play.
This helps me convey what I wish to say.
I add characters, settings and imagination.
And with a bit of free licence, some exaggeration.
Then I take my script to a group who perform.
And the words I have written, they physically transform.
I am a playwright pursuing my dreams.
Like you, I'm in demand. Or that's how it seems.
I feel no pressure to write the next play,
As I experience new joys at different places I stay.
But what's happening this time, meeting with you,
Means the next time I write it will all be true.
As you could paint me and set imagination free,
I could write beautiful scripts about you and me.
The flow and majesty of our coming together.
The ease with which we made each other feel better.
I can already see the opening act.
Two beach-loving souls and how they come to attract.
How they were feeling when day gave birth to night.
The inescapable truth of love at first sight.
To capture these moments and place them on a stage,
Would mark my work with a coming of age."
The whirlwind of love they now found themselves in,

Was controlling their feelings and making them spin.
They had taken a step further down an unknown path.
As they looked at each other they began to laugh.
They sensed this advance in a unified way.
A layer had peeled and simply flew away.
So now they knew something that set the other alive.
If they had one thing in common, it was passionate drive.
Like a goddess of Olympia or an angel in the sky.
She saw her own Adonis as she looked him in the eye.
Breathing free expression. She could not be more relaxed.
Numbing with the feeling of being pleasantly attached.
All her senses, now turned on, were in a place so high.
A flood of love ran through her soul. She released an easy
sigh.
He felt like a lord, who served the court of King Arthur.
Or the head of a legion from, the once mighty, Sparta.
He emanated empowerment, over him and him alone.
Standing there, with her at his side, he had found a brand-
new home.
"Monique," he said, with his arm round her shoulder.
"Shall we go for a walk before the day grows older?
We can stroll round the town and appreciate its beauty.
I'll shower you with love as though it were my duty."
He shut up shop. They set off for a stroll.
Stopped in the market to buy soup and a bread roll.
The narrow streets with their shops and the odd little stall,
Were gazed upon gently by the towering church hall.
A perfect backdrop against the town's small valleys,
As the lowering sun found its way through the alleys.
Monique couldn't stop smiling as joy welled within her.
"This is a perfect place for you to take me to dinner."

Chapter 3

The waiter lit the candle in an atmosphere divine.
Gave them both a pleasant smile as he uncorked a bottle of wine.
He politely poured their drinks. Nodded and moved away.
Allowing them to enjoy, the end of a wonderful day.
Their table was on a veranda. Looking down upon the town.
Dusk set a tone of love, in which they felt they both could drown.
Monique rested her elbow on the arm of her chair.
Ran her fingers slowly, through her soft and silky hair.
"This is nice," she said, as lanterns gave a radiant glow.
Like pendulums on grandfather clocks, moving to and fro.
And the comfort of silence one can have with a friend,
Warmed Monique as it did slowly descend.
Leon looked at her and it could clearly be seen.
Behind vacant eyes, she was in a daydream.
She could see white petals falling as she looked at the skies.
Resting on the shoulders of people with smiles.
Familiar faces with hearts full of love.
And a man releasing a single dove.
The edges of the scene were slightly blurred.
Cheers and laughter were clearly heard.

Blossom from trees. A pink blanket on the ground.
Monique in tears. Her ears were drowned.
Leon's arm around her and a feeling so well.
Two characters in a fairytale who were under a spell.
Not far behind her she could hear a choir sing.
Church bells shuddered through her, with every single ring.
She was so overcome with a deep sense of pride.
For, as she looked at herself, she was dressed as a bride.
When she returned to the table from the place she had been,
She was speechless with joy as if still in the dream.
The waiter placed menus at each of their sides.
Monique suppressed feelings she could barely hide.
How could she express what just happened in her mind?
Too soon to mention. Perhaps, another time.
"Well Monique, what on earth can I say?
You must have seen something in a special way.
I've just sat and watched you drift on by.
At one point you nearly had tears in your eye.
When I see someone daydreaming, I leave them be.
And I would love to see what they can see.
You can tell me one time, when you feel it is right.
Though, I do not imagine you will tell me tonight.
When I say this, I say it with a loving intent.
There is a very large part of me that can sense where you
went."
He raised his eyebrows once and gave a shy smile.
He'd not felt this embarrassed for a while.
They found time for a laugh as their eyes met again.
"Oh, forget this wine," he said. "Let's have champagne!"
They ordered their food and it was all so lovely.
Fuzziness took over as they finished the bubbly.

So, arm in arm, they walked down the street.
With that slightly drunk feeling that takes over one's feet.
He grabbed her middle with both his hands.
She screamed then laughed and called him a clown.
It was so much fun. The laughs were aplenty.
They could have fooled anyone they were under twenty.
The church clock sounded the midnight bell.
As they walked up the steps of a lavish hotel.
He purchased some items and, for her, a small nightie.
A perfect size that would not fit too tightly.
They stepped out of the lift and went into their suite.
Leon slumped in a chair to take a load off his feet.
Monique went to the bathroom and took off her clothes.
Held the nightie to her chest and made a provocative pose.
She slipped it on. It barely reached her thighs.
How naughty she felt. Even through her eyes.
She entered the room and climbed on the bed.
Excited thoughts running through her head.
She lay on her side. Not wanting sleep just now.
A little goddess, so still, in her satin gown.
He removed all his clothes. He had a smile on his face.
She reminded him of the woman who was covered in lace.
She felt his presence, just there, behind her.
Her dazzling beauty a constant reminder.
He thought, *I am so grateful that she warms to me.*
He whispered her name so her face he could see.
She turned her head round for their eyes to meet.
He placed his hands at the top of her feet.
She turned away, chuckling like a child.
As he moved up her shin, she could not stop the smiles.
He moved onto the bed and carbon-copied her position.

Stroking her thigh in one smooth transition.
Her nightdress rode high to reveal her bare cheeks.
He caressed gently higher as she lay on the sheets.
His hand moved round, just below her breast.
He slid it up through the middle of her chest.
Her arm glided round and rested on his knee.
Pulling him to her for a more passionate feel.
His pulsating love touched her smooth, warm skin.
His lips kissed her neck. Such a beautiful thing.
His soft, inner forearm brushed her stiffened nipples.
Her legs clamped together as she shivered in ripples.
He moved over her breasts as soft as he could.
The very tips of his fingers as a blind man would.
He kissed the back of her arm. Rubbed the side of her neck.
She looked close to orgasm when he glanced to check.
He breathed warm air on the middle of her spine.
Felt her legs tremble. He knew it was time.
He placed the tip of his tongue on her soft, silk skin.
Moved slowly down as she said that she loved him.
He was curled in a ball as he met the top of her peach.
She moaned with sheer pleasure. Felt she could weep.
He looked at her. It was a picture of love.
She smiled and rolled over as her legs opened up.
Slowly. Tenderly. He kissed the inside of her leg.
She was alive as she felt his breath.
He dragged his wet tongue through the slightest of hair.
She removed her garment so she was totally bare.
He reached her other leg and let out a small sigh.
As he gazed up, they met eye-to-eye.
She nodded twice for him to advance.
Then grabbed his head in both her hands.

And plunged him to her as she could wait no more.
This is what love was created for.
His arms wrapped round her legs with tight intention.
They opened even further. Almost beyond comprehension.
Delicately, he let her feel him right there.
As he began to French-kiss her with all of his care.
With both his hands he reached for her breasts.
Her body was shaking as she drew short breaths.
Her legs shuddered hard. She let go a groan.
He continued intensely to the sound of her moan.
Her feet on the bed. Her body arced in a crescent.
Spasmodic orgasm was clearly present.
She slumped on the bed, tingling all over.
At that point in time, he knew he must hold her.
So, he quickly moved up and grabbed her tight.
Her shaking hands were a wonderful sight.
He kissed her and she was lost in herself.
They were completely full of sexual wealth.
She then lay on her front. His hands slid down her thighs.
The look of love lay deep in their eyes.
She wanted him to lie on her so they could not be closer.
He honoured the invite and placed himself on her.
Their bodies, arms and legs touched each other's.
A spiritual feeling ran through two lovers.
They savoured all moments. He needed her kiss.
As his love rested gently in her beautiful crevice.
He clutched her tight and rolled right over.
She lay, facing away. Her head rested on his shoulder.
His hands ran up her ribs with the slightest of force.
The sound she made was a little hoarse.
He held her breasts. Her nipples were red.

All of his love lay here in this bed.
The fronts of his knees met the back of hers.
He lifted them up to admire her curves.
He opened his legs so hers were ajar.
More pleasure waited. They knew it was not far.
He slid his hand down between her legs.
Left it there as he kissed her neck.
She rolled her hips to move his love around.
Now it was him making a groaning sound.
He could feel her. He could touch her. He wanted her so bad.
This was the most exciting feeling he'd ever had.
As he did to her, she made him wait.
She wanted him in the most heightened state.
Her hands moved down and grabbed at his side.
He was dizzy with lust that he could not hide.
She pushed herself down, hard against him.
Not letting him enter or allowing him to begin.
She wanted him in a frenzied condition.
He grabbed her middle to try and end her mission.
Her warm hand slid between her legs.
She took hold of him where he was tense.
Rubbing back and forth in such a slow fashion.
She could not have added any more passion.
Then she guided his love, slowly in.
Just a little, for now, and he was tingling.
Then out again. She liked to be teased.
How nice it was as they were both so pleased.
Once more he was in and he travelled deep.
Her hands moved away and rested on the sheet.
Palms on the bed. She rotated her hips.
Her love wrapped around him. He felt her grip.

She then changed her position and thrust up and down.
Aggressive jerks and a sexy growl.
His excitement was rising. He needed her to slow up.
Wanting the moment to last. He had a full cup.
He grabbed her hips. Pulled her down to a halt.
A scream of pleasure. Her body did jolt.
She lay flat on him. He began to thrust.
Slow and easy. He was full of lust.
Her legs either side of him. Tensed so much.
Their hands clasped together in a tight, loving touch.
He moved as quick as he could, wanting to give her his all.
She gyrated frantically out of control.
With a final push, he lifted her right off the bed.
A rush of blood shot to the top of his head.
His warm love exploded deep inside.
He cried out her name at the end of the ride.
They were soaked in sweat from head to toe.
A perfect expression as they both let go.
He crossed his arms over the front of her chest.
Ecstatically shaking and staggered breaths.
"Oh Monique, I'm vibrating in-love at the highest degree.
I never knew I could feel this free.
I could hold you here till the end of time.
I will be yours if you will be mine.
I could love you forever if you would permit.
The fire inside me, you have lit.
The feelings I have are ever so empowering.
The fruit of my love will be eternally flowering.
When I first saw you appear on the sand.
I knew that love was holding my hand."
He moved one arm. They rolled onto their side.

He had more feelings to share that he could not hide.
He pulled up the duvet to cover them both.
Then, in her ear, he gently spoke.
"You are the one I have fallen in love with.
All that I have, to you, I would give.
We could travel together to all sorts of places.
Sun-soaked beaches or a day at the races.
I can just see you now in your summer clothes.
One elbow on your knee, in a thoughtful pose.
It's a warm, summer day with blue skies above.
You and I floating. Completely in-love.
I love your warm skin when it touches mine.
Nothing else matters. Not even time.
You make love so passionately. Not the least bit afraid.
It's like a journey through an ocean with a beautiful mermaid.
Can you feel where we're going? Does it excite your soul?
Do you, like me, feel completely whole?
I could tell you I love you forever and a day.
Three words, I love you, I'd never tire to say.
I love you Monique. The words roll off my tongue.
You could make my heart feel forever young.
I have never said this in my entire life.
I'm in love with the idea of you being my wife.
What do you think? Shall we make it come true?
You've said that you love me, and I love you.
Were you dreaming of a wedding earlier tonight?
When a girl has that look it's a beautiful sight.
It could be a grand event with family and friends.
On a journey of love that never ends.
Then we could sail away for a wonderful cruise.
Just you and I on a honeymoon.

And upon the deck, neath the starry skies.
The moon would reflect off your sparkly, blue eyes.
Your bright, warm smile framed by a low-cut dress,
Having me swear I was with a princess.
We could listen to the waves whilst they sing their song.
As the freedom of love just carried us along.
With stop-offs and visits to exotic ports.
Sampling delights of all kinds and sorts.
Eating fresh fish just caught from the beaches.
By locals in far-off Caribbean reaches.
We could hire a small boat and set off for the day.
In search of our very own secluded little bay.
Just you and I together, hand in hand.
With the cover of some rocks we'd make love on the sand.
Swim in the clear ocean. Hold one another.
With no-one around to blow our cover.
We could then journey home and find a place to stay.
Close to the actors who perform your plays.
I could sit and watch your magic unfold.
A silent witness to your stories told.
I would kiss, love and be there for you.
Support your work for your dreams to come true."
He lifted his head to take a little peek.
Smiled as he saw Monique was asleep.
"Oh well," he said, as he stroked her hair.
"I guess that was a moment we're not ready to share."
He rolled onto his back. His hands clasped his head.
Thoughts of a future filling his head.
He found a smile and he had a quick laugh,
As he wondered to himself, where next on this path?

Chapter 4

Monique was dreaming of a distant land.
An ocean island with golden sand.
She walked with Leon along the beach.
Lost in love and out of reach.
Only two sets of footprints ever graced this shore.
This was their Eden for them to explore.
They were as free as they could possibly be.
Their feet felt the warmth of the crystal-clear sea.
The sun warmed their skin and shone through the leaves.
As they stepped in and out, the shadow of palm trees.
There was a multitude of colour to admire.
Which made the feeling of love much higher.
The sound from the jungle was a beautiful chorus.
Monique thought, *Orchestral earth plays this harmony for us.*
They stopped. They turned to each other.
Monique felt a wave of love rush through her.
With a smile on her face she simply said, "Yes."
Her heart opened up. She was about to undress.
When it fell to the ground and lay on the sand.
Leon threw off his clothes and grabbed her hand.
He pulled her naked body to his.
She put her hand on his chest to control his bliss.

Not yet, was the signal. She meant no harm.
She let go of his hand and linked his arm.
They carried on lazily, down the coast.
So relaxed and as warm as toast.
The sense of freedom was completely unbounded.
The feelings within were so well-rounded.
An opening appeared at the jungle's edge.
So, with curious minds and tender steps,
They entered in and were so overcome.
The beauty of nature's work had been done.
With the excitement of children at seaside fairs,
They climbed a tree and picked at some pears.
As the juices ran down her beautiful face.
He breathed her nakedness at a quickened pace.
Her soul was so soft and very calm.
He climbed from the tree and held out his arm.
She floated down, as though on a slide.
Into his clutch she did gently glide.
A moment was found to kiss each other's lips.
She silhouetted the sun in a human eclipse.
She was coursing with love through her very being.
Completely transfixed. He was all she was seeing.
He sensed her emotion and placed a palm on her cheek.
Through daydream eyes he did softly speak.
"Patience my love, for you know how I feel.
Let us search our Eden and make it our meal.
Let us not rush this moment for all shall be well.
For when we are ready the feelings will tell.
The thirst of your love, I soon will water.
For you are my goddess. You are Earth's daughter."
Her breath was completely taken away,

As a fanfare sounded for her this day.
So they made their way to a beautiful clearing.
The vision they beheld was so endearing.
Smooth rocks, a pool and birds singing out loud.
She felt so blessed by their heavenly sound.
With the sun at its back a waterfall fell.
A rainbow emerged that looked so well.
They dived in the water and swam its breadth.
Felt the excitement of its unknown depth.
They stood on the rocks and showered in the fall.
Invigorated fully by the cool water-wall.
They stepped out of the rush of the falling wet.
A time neither one of them could ever forget.
They lay on silk rocks. The sun burst through the trees,
As it found a hole through the green canopies.
Her arms and her body were fully outstretched.
He lay at her side and admired her breasts.
He stared through her eyes to the core of her soul.
She struggled to grasp. She was losing control.
Lost in his eyes. She needed his kiss.
Every cell in her body overflowed with bliss.
He invited her to him with open arms.
She was moved elsewhere by his warming charms.
They made love in the sun. Nothing short of artistic.
Every touch and kiss felt so realistic.
They then lay on their backs at each other's side.
Drawing short breaths to let the feelings subside.
The sun fell away behind the cover of trees.
He sat upright. She was between his knees.
She peered at the sky and alone and afar.
She smiled to herself as she saw the first star.

The whole scene started melting and began to swirl.
Monique felt vulnerable, as though she were a little girl.
She was tumbling and twisting and slightly scared.
Her eyes blinked rapidly. Her vision was impaired.
Then all of a sudden, she felt a breeze on her cheek.
Her feet landed softly in a field of wheat.
Leon was there, standing in the sun.
Another part of her dream had now begun.
She took his hand in a delicate way.
Looked in his eyes and heard herself say,
"Let that summer feeling fill our souls.
Shall we run through the fields and lose control?
Let's laugh together. Get excited as we can.
Show our joy and not give a damn.
Today is here and we are alive.
Let's enjoy one another through each other's eyes.
Forget all our tomorrows, for their time will come.
Let us love each other in the summer sun.
Can I hold you, my love, with your face in my palms?
May I kiss your lips whilst wrapped in your arms?
I want to blot out everything but you.
So your face is the only thing shining through.
Shall we put on our bathers and swim in the river?
Frolic like otters hither and thither.
The sun can dry us after our dip.
We can open a basket and have a picnic.
A sandwich or two. A cream cake to follow.
A bottle of champagne for us to swallow.
Say, "Cheers!" to our love and a very nice time.
I'll kiss you gently to make you feel fine.
We can lie in a meadow and smile at it all.

Shrug off our cares. Be completely enthralled.
Have the time of our lives, where we are together.
All else can dissolve as we lay in the heather.
Let's make this day ours, to experience all joy.
Let's make this day ours, just you and me boy.
Or we could go to the seaside. A place we both like.
Roll down the promenade on a hired bike.
Hear the sound of the waves from the ocean's din.
Where the salted air can find our skin.
We can delight in all of the coastal thrills.
Find a place to make love, up in the sand-hills.
Get some ice-cream covered in raspberry sauce.
Sprinkled crushed nuts on the top, of course.
We can lie on the sand and bathe in the day.
The sea air can blow all our cobwebs away.
Smiles all around for the love we have found.
Put shells to our ears and hear their sound.
Right there I shall hold you as you look at me,
As we marvel at the flow of the mighty sea.
I can talk about how much I feel for you,
As we take in the calmness of the sandy sea view.
We can listen to seagulls cry out their sound,
In their endless quest to find food on the ground.
You can tell me you love me as we lay by each other.
I'll do the same, my beautiful lover.
And when the hot sun falls from the skies.
We can go skinny-dipping once the moon does arise.
Under the moonlight I will glance in your eye.
Right there in the sea I will make you mine.
I wish all days were ours to enjoy in this way.
If they were, I know, it's with you I would play."

Then her dream began to shift once more.
Until she was stood in front of an open door.
She crossed its threshold. Leon was there.
Looking right at her from a reclining chair.
She could see his lips moving but no sound came from him.
She edged slowly closer to try to tune in.
He was talking gently. It was something romantic.
She sat on his lap. Completely enchanted.
She lay on his chest. He embraced her body.
His words were like music as he whispered them softly.
"There is a feeling like no other,
Which comes to you, through your lover.
Your soul explodes from tip to toe.
A state that every human should know.
It's the highest point of a wonderful time.
When it finds you, your heart will chime.
It brushes your strings. It sings like a lark.
As though one of God's angels was playing a harp.
The lift it gives has no contest.
How can it, when your love's at your breast?
Twixt in the grip of the one you love.
Blissfully serene. Tranquil as the dove.
Time stands still. Nothing else can count.
Where your lovers' joy becomes paramount.
I live for me. I live for you.
A supreme sensation, of love, that is true.
Wrapped around you. Lost in your grace.
I could cry with love when I gaze at your face.
My senses climb. I let go of resolve.
The strength of our love can only evolve.
This heart could burst into a million pieces.

They'd all sound your name with divine completeness.
I would bring them all back to your warmth and your heat.
There we would wait, bowed at your feet.
You consume my thoughts at the moment I wake.
My heartbeat quickens. My body does shake.
I draw short breaths with you in my mind.
Your angelic presence, to me, is so fine.
Suspended, in-love, when I bask in your rays.
You're the sun that shines through me for all of my days.
When your hands are in mine, I walk on my path.
In a celestial city with no need to look back.
You are the key to all of my doors.
For you are mine and I am yours.
As, together, we walk on this beautiful road.
Of unfolding love that cannot be foretold.
Blessed by your touch and your sweet caress.
I'm in a higher place when I see you undress.
With your naked body pressed to mine.
Interwoven together in a human entwine.
And there we are, adoring each other.
As we melt into one, my perfect lover.
When our lips meet for a tender kiss.
I overflow and nothing's amiss.
Know, when I kiss you, I give all my desire.
Adorned with your passion. My body on fire.
When your eyes are closed, you look so far gone.
Let me take you, my love, to Avalon.
Then we make love and freedom reigns.
Exquisite expression and euphoric gains.
When your love speaks, it rings all around.
I succumb unto you and your heavenly sound.

Your warm breaths are rapid. Your body is taut.
As we cling to each other. Gripped by love's claws.
Through these eyes I look at you,
With always the freshness of morning dew.
My angels sing a harmonious song,
As they carry my love with their mighty throng.
I kiss you all over for our love rendition.
Your body shivers in sensual submission.
With the slightest touch, you let my hands slide.
Upon your nakedness I gently glide.
I know your body as much as my own.
My fountain of love, for you, has so grown.
Without you, where would I be?
A ship with no rudder, lost on the sea.
I would be torn asunder if we were apart.
Your love would hang heavy upon my heart.
I would fall to my knees as I would miss your embrace.
And the day would see my tear-stained face.
My arms outstretched as I looked at the sky.
This love for you will never die.
For you are my all. You're the air in me.
Unconditional love, I have only for thee.
Eternally honoured by your radiant flow.
A feeling, till now, I had never known.
So I thank you, my love, for fantastic you.
As all of my dreams begin to come true.
I have a word. It's the best of them all.
It's bigger than anything and yet, so small.
It's the conqueror of everything. A feeling within.
'Tis the master of the universe. An eloquent thing.
It's the centre of the earth to way up above.

It's my feeling for you. The word is love.
I love your warm breath in my face when we kiss.
Your tender touch. Your moistened lips.
I love brushing your cheek with the back of my hand.
So smooth and inviting like golden sand.
I love hearing your voice and talking with you.
Whatever you want, you could have me do.
I love who you are and the way you live.
The joy you bring. The love you give.
I love being with you all of the time.
And the way you tip-toe round my mind.
I love you in my thoughts when I close my eyes.
It fills my heart and lights up the skies.
I love when you laugh. The sound is just right.
When we laugh together it is pure delight.
I love your aroma, moving around me.
Glad you and I can feel this free.
I love your face. It is a picture to behold.
Like summer flowers that light up the meadows.
I love that we could walk hand in hand.
Along beaches, barefoot, on sea-soaked sand.
I love the feelings I have when in bed you slide.
As we lay looking at each other side-by-side.
I love your sexual expression when you completely let go,
As you and I connect in the exact same flow.
I love everything about you. This much is true.
You already know I am in love with you."
These were dreams, unmatched by all others.
Monique was floating beneath the covers.
The pictures in her head were fantasies to feel.
Subconscious freedom. Ever so real.

Deep in sleep, she was living each scene.
Miles away. Sailing on a dream.
Rapid eye movement as her eyelids fluttered.
Striking images. Completely uncluttered.
She was in utopia, which heaven could only know.
No actors here. She was the star of the show.
There were a hundred places her dream did go.
Each as joyous as the last, for her to know.
Her heart was full. She was highly turned on.
Flying to places that were so far gone.
Her legs and her arms were clutching the duvet.
Saddling pleasure as her dream moved in new ways.
She was making love like never before.
Inside paradise, on every shore.
Dreams of heaven ran through her brain.
The heart of love pulsed in every vein.
Her waking time was being reflected here.
Undistorted beauty. Evidently clear.
She looked in mirrors at her naked self.
Smiling back in the best of health.
She heard a sound. It was her name being spoken.
Slowly, but surely, she was being awoken.
She had been dreaming of the best of times.
As now, the morning sun burst through the blinds.
She opened her eyes with no clue where she'd been.
As the door of unconsciousness closed on her dream.

Chapter 5

"Good morning my love. How do you fair?"

He was sat at her side stroking her hair.

She said, "I don't know what happened from last night until now.

But what I do know is I love you more, somehow.

I have a familiar feeling that clarifies my sight.

When this happens, I am compelled to write."

She sat up in bed. In her throat was a lump.

Shivering as her body became covered in goose-bumps.

"The time is right now. I must get dressed.

I have to go. I will write down my address."

"Monique, what do you mean? I don't understand."

He looked in her eyes as he grabbed her hand.

"Leon, please do not fret. Just let me explain.

I have a thousand ideas exploding through my brain.

You know I love you. That will not cease.

I need you to accept I need solitude and peace."

He turned around and put his face in his hands.

He had to be the person who most understands.

He said, "OK, OK. Let me just take this in.

I know what you mean but where do I begin?"

He was clearly disturbed from this instant upheaval.

But, somehow, he knew of her internal ordeal.
He said, "I know when I paint, I must be alone.
I go to the place of my inner home.
I know you need time in order to create.
My only wish is your love will not dissipate.
Can you leave me a number, that I may give you a ring?
Or will you take mine? Please take that one thing?"
She looked at his face. A tear rolled down his cheek.
She threw her arms and legs round him then began to speak.
"This is not goodbye. It is a short farewell.
You must see through my eyes in order to tell.
When I look at you my heart is so full.
I could see grey skies and they would never be dull.
Just stay in-love with me. I'll be your eternal rose.
I will forever lie at the end of your rainbows.
For you are all of those colours when seen from this soul.
So always know this is the heart you stole."
"Yes Monique, I am on your side.
I know, for you, I must lay down my pride.
For, pride prevents progress in so many things.
I do not want the feelings that that behaviour brings.
I know it is farewell until the time is right.
That comfort I will take to my bed each night.
I do ask one honour that I may hear from your lips.
May I read what you've written when you finish your script?"
"Leon, believe me, you will be the first to know.
There is no one else I would rather show.
But I must be gone as soon as I can.
To catch the next flight to Amsterdam.
I have a four-storey house in a nice part of the city.
It's painted brightly. It's ever so pretty.

That's where I go when I need to write.
The view from my window is a heavenly sight.
Trams pass by. I just love to see them.
They stop over the road near the Van Gogh museum.
Will you come to the terminal to see me away?
I'll call a cab. We can chat on the way."
The taxi arrived and set off to the airport.
They never spoke as they were lost in thought.
Monique was seeing the play she would write.
Leon peered out the window with a look of fright.
They were in different places as the journey went on.
He was struggling with the truth that she'd soon be gone.
It was like a clip from a movie of slow-motion scene.
Where the characters look lost and all seems like a dream.
In her hand was a ticket. She stopped and turned round.
As she stood at the entrance of the departure lounge.
She said, "Well, this is it! For now, it's goodbye,"
As water welled up and filled her eye.
"Monique, can I steal a kiss before you go?
Though, I dare not hold you as I might not let go."
She put her hand on his cheek. Their lips lightly met.
He clung to the moment so he would not forget.
She placed a piece of paper in the palm of his hand.
"That's my cell-phone number and my address in
Amsterdam."
"Goodbye Monique. Tell me we will meet again.
If only to alleviate some of the pain."
"We will, I swear. Of that I am certain.
You'll have the best seat in the house when they raise the
curtain.
Goodbye Leon. You just make sure you phone.

I'll need the lift when I am sat all alone."
She turned to the attendant and showed her card.
Though, she could not look back. That was too hard.
Leon felt like he'd been steamrolled as soon as she'd gone.
The pain inside was like the death of a loved one.
His stomach turned over. He was clearly sad.
This was the most heart-breaking feeling he'd had.
He bought a coffee and found a chair.
Feelings took over that were beyond compare.
He stretched out his legs. He knew he needed to be strong.
Whenever he was down, he was not down for long.
He focused on love as he breathed in and out.
And from doing this a good feeling came about.
He knew he loved her and that she loved him.
He had the urge to paint. He knew where to begin.
He could already see it without painting a stroke.
Like musicians who hear music as they write down each note.
In the blink of an eye his chair became vacant.
Soon he'd make real, that which was latent.
He hailed a taxi and set off for home.
Inside his mind a masterpiece had grown.
He got to his house and went to a room in the back,
To remove a canvas from the large storage rack.
He took the biggest there was and wrangled it on a stand.
Picked out some pencils to get the outline planned.
For seven hours he stood there and drew.
The acorn in his mind was now on view.
He put down his pencil and moved away,
To see his creation as if it was on display.
At this black and white stage, it looked rather quaint.
Tomorrow he would begin to add the paint.

He closed the door, then went to bed.
With positive thoughts running through his head.
He lay for a moment looking at the picture called "She."
Right at that time all sadness was set free.
His old friend tiredness came and lay at his side,
As the blanket of night helped close his eyes.
He rose in the morning and made a hot drink.
Closed his eyes and started to think.
He made a huffing sound, knowing why he was low.
Trying to support the fact she'd had to go.
He thought, *All things are difficult before they are easy.*
A sobering truth that left him, somewhat, queasy.
He had that unsettling feeling, so hard to translate.
Like a part of his soul knew it could suffocate.
In a few short days he could not believe what had passed.
He'd scaled the highs. Then all around him had collapsed.
Alone but not lonely because he always had his thoughts.
But they were generating feelings of unwelcome sorts.
His body ached. His teeth became clenched.
His mind rolled in circles. His gut was wrenched.
He thought, *When do I call her? When will we speak?*
Do I leave it a few days or as much as a week?
I miss her already. It's only been a day.
I feel like I've lost her now she's gone away.
And as the mind can, it started adding more doubt.
Inside his head he began to scream and shout.
The voice that was guiding his every decision,
Was taking control with sinister precision.
His internal dialogue was sending him down.
Right to the point where he was wearing a frown.
He thought, *To hell with this! I need the outdoors.*

I'll go for a walk along the shores.
He strolled to the beach and took some long, deep breaths.
Trying to dissolve these new-born depths.
There were very few people taking a walk.
Just what he needed to gather his thoughts.
Whenever he felt lost this was where he came.
The place excused, from any or all blame.
He always found a truth that met a resounding end.
Where emotion tackled reality and neither dare pretend.
His feet hit the sand. He stood still for an instant.
The magnitude of the vastness made his plight seem
insignificant.
She fell into his mind as he looked down at the sand.
He closed his eyes and imagined holding her hand.
Her untouchable beauty caressed his mind.
The break of each wave was perfectly timed.
A moment of clarity drifted down from above.
He thought, *Now I can see through your eyes, my love.*
He breathed the sea air without a single care.
Now relieved of discomfort and reprieved of despair.
Have faith, he thought, *in that which is unseen.*
Embark on the belief and the reality of a dream.
So, he pictured her sitting and writing her words.
Imagining his soul drifting into hers.
The magic he produced felt like a spiritual levitation.
Calmness crept through him with the peace of a meditation.
A sensation came about that began in his feet.
Gathering momentum like a wave to a beach.
Then that feeling one gets that climbs up the spine,
Which strikes through the heart at the very same time.
It arrived without asking like someone making a surprise visit.

Far from far-flung, it was inwardly exquisite.
It was completely earth-shaking like a geyser's boom.
It flared into the world like a Rio-dancer's plume.
This wonderful constant was totally undisturbed.
The energy he gave off was calm and unperturbed.
He thought, *If I can experience this, then love is real.*
I may not touch or see it, but it's something I feel.
Then he opened his eyes. His whole being felt lighter.
The blue sky, sea and sand all seemed a lot brighter.
He took it all in as he started to walk.
Inside his head he began to talk.
Now that feels better. I can see more clearly.
I needed a reminder that I love her dearly.
I hope she's well and had a pleasant flight.
That put her in a mind to creatively write.
He floated along with a sparkle in his eye.
Enthusiastically greeted a passer-by.
The paces were quick. He strode with delight.
His feelings had certainly taken flight.
The air became fresher and seemed even more salted.
He was placed in a state nothing short of exalted.
His soul was in-love. It was singing its song.
Ever-quicker, he moved along.
For every breath of his life, he only wanted to love her.
Everything about her, he'd be glad to discover.
He felt each passing second. His pulse pounded in his ears.
Never, had he experienced this in all his years.
He stopped, exhausted. Not realising he'd been running.
His creative juices were vibrantly pumping.
He knew this was the time to craft his creation.
Right now while his soul was in a state of elevation.

He thought, *I must get back and start with the brush.*
Turning around quickly, he began to rush.
Halfway back, he became even more excited.
A thought crossed his mind that made him highly delighted.
He noticed how the urge stood beyond any other thing.
So he stopped whilst the sentiment was lingering.
He laughed out loud and held a Cheshire-Cat grin.
What had happened to Monique had now happened to him.
He dropped his shoulders and bowed his head,
As empathy covered him like butter to bread.
He thought, *I now understand my resistance was in vain.*
Would heaven or earth stop me and start to complain?
As I must now paint. She had to go and write.
When inspiration beckons, it uses all its might.
We cannot cast it off. It would be crazy to ignore.
It is what she and I were put on this planet for.
Passing through the door, he entered the back room.
He closed the door as if sealing a tomb.
A poignant few seconds as he scanned what he'd sketched.
The perfect translation, from his mind, had been etched.
He closed his eyes and breathed pure love in.
To clear his thoughts as he was about to begin.
All he could see was the resulting image.
He felt it. He breathed it. Its depth had no limit.
He picked up his palette and took out a brush.
His work had begun. He now had the rush.
He looked deep in his heart. It mirrored a reflection.
What flowed through the brush was a beautiful projection.
The hours seemed like seconds. He was deep in a trance.
Upon the canvas his brush did dance.
The day grew long in no time at all.

He knew this would sit comfortably on a large, white wall.
He snapped out of the zone where time has no say.
Closed his eyes tight as they were stinging away.
He blinked a few times but would not stand back and look.
That would be like prematurely reading the last page of a
book.
He knew where it was and where it needed to be.
It could only be appreciated in its entirety.
He put his things down and left the room for the day.
Then picked out some soothing music to play.
A classical piece with lots of flowing strings.
That filled his mind with many beautiful things.
Then he closed his eyes and hugged his own body.
Swayed side to side as the sounds played softly.
He was holding her close, and she too him.
Reassuring warmth came from within.
He spoke out loud as if she were there.
With absolutely no need to care.
"Monique, my love, this is really so nice.
I see us like skaters, performing on ice.
We're twisting and turning so close together.
Synchronicity flourishing, for us to be in forever.
Come with me, my love. We can dance on the night.
Drift through the stars in carefree flight.
Love can be the wind that fills our sails up.
We can taste the elixir from the everlasting cup.
I will be your king for you are my queen.
Together, we can fly to the edge of a dream."
He carried these thoughts and many more,
As he moved here and there around the floor.
He was completely gone. He bumped into a chair.

His eyes now open, he had that daydream stare.
The music had stopped. He did not hear its end.
Another day had gone by without his best friend.
It was time to sleep. The day had made him tire.
He lay down his head. He was full of desire.
He looked at the candle, all melted, on the bottle.
It was like an exhausted volcano after erupting full-throttle.
His mind's eye showed him pictures of a naked Monique.
She had verve as she moved. She was very chic.
She looked attractive as she danced in his head.
As relaxation swept right through his bed.
His body felt numb, but his mind did not.
The efforts of the day, he soon forgot.
Tomorrow, a new day. A new start. A fresh approach.
More magic to be born with every one of his strokes.
But he was content, thus far, with his ongoing achievement.
As her slipping away seemed less like bereavement.
He still pained to be with her but accepted life's flow.
He was coming to terms with the status quo.
His respect for her needs was way beyond immense.
He thought, *When love is parted, its lessons are intense.*
He refused to donate or entertain ill-will.
She was everything he dreamed of. Not some bitter pill.
He lay on his back and blew out all his air.
As a baptism of knowledge made him more aware.
If one of them was Yin then the other must be Yang.
An enriching premise for him to understand.
He adored these new thoughts as they were so unregimented.
Previous boundaries, pushed further, were now far more
augmented.
Good thoughts and feelings all the way,

Gave him a concrete reason to smile at each day.

He had an enhanced feeling of total self-worth.

The recent transformation was a welcomed rebirth.

He woke the next morning and wanted to get straight to work.

But first, a large coffee to give him a perk.

He sat at the breakfast bar. His fist propped his cheek.

The love inside, had him dwell on Monique.

He guessed a day or two and the piece would be finished.

The creativity he was experiencing would soon be diminished.

That very thought prompted him to get to his feet.

He then made the decision to not stop till it was complete.

For a whole day and a night, he carried on painting.

Fatigue, eventually, had him hallucinating.

Then it was done. His brush moved to the right corner.

He wrote his moniker, and with a name he would adorn her.

To the left he moved and as this was like no other.

He painted the two words "Beautiful lover."

He walked away so he could see it as it should be.

This was now the time to appreciate its entirety.

As with his usual approach, the image was unconventional.

When viewed from further back it appeared three-dimensional.

It was Monique and her eyes were closed.

Her lips were full and as red as a rose.

Her mouth was open as if she were breathing life.

An uplifting image, like seeing a leading light.

Her cheekbones were proud. A look of the highest grace.

Perfectly balanced on her slim, tapered face.

Her arms were outstretched. Slightly angled to the stars.

Like a gymnast acknowledging before they start.

She wore a translucent white gown with a loop for each finger.
This fanned out like wings either side of her figure.
An exploding sun, from behind, almost shone right through.
White light-beams at all angles like luminous chutes.
Such depths in the background with visions of hope.
Like sneaking a peek through a space telescope.
Shimmering pink clouds and endless star systems.
Each demanding attention like questions from children.
At her feet lay a figure. It was a single soul.
Light came from it of the purest gold.
Her presence was giving joy to this individual.
Profiting, thankfully, in her energetic residual.
A person may get lost in this picture for much time.
It could push them to the edge of their perceiving mind.
It borderlined biblical in its brilliant portrayal.
A piece he would be happy and proud to unveil.
But this was not a painting for the highest bidder.
Selling it was something he would not consider.
It was a gift of love. An offering from his heart.
A masterstroke of expression that he was compelled to impart.
It had flamboyance and panache. It radiated élan.
This, he must send to Amsterdam.
The morning sun dragged itself into the skies.
Softly shining in his tired eyes.
Then a ritual he performed after each work of art.
Cognac over ice and a Cuban cigar.
He stood in front of it, swirling his glass.
Knowing this painting was in another class.
He drew on his cigar as he stared at her lips.

Thinking to himself, *Did I really do this?*
He exhaled smoke away from the painting.
This was something he did not want tainting.

Chapter 6

Shook by the disturbance from a knock at the door.
A face appeared from the window of the high fourth floor.
"Give me a minute. I'm on my way down."
Monique had been daydreaming as she gazed across town.
Two weeks had passed since they had last spoken.
Something inside her was to be re-awoken.
How time can distort someone's looks in your mind.
Where you have to dig deep, for a clear image to find.
And needing the freshness of their face again,
To be nicely imprinted at the front of your brain.
She got to the door and undid the locks.
On her doorstep were two men with a slim, wooden box.
"Hello Miss, is your name Monique?"
"Yes," she replied. "I guess that box is for me?"
"It is. It says to be handled delicately.
Special delivery. Sent from Italy."
She shivered down her back. It was something from Leon.
"Could you place it in my front room before you are gone?"
She signed their note and gave them ten euros.
They thanked her, and were off, as the front door was closed.
She got some scissors and cut through the straps.
Then gently unlocked the metal clasps.

It was five feet tall and as equally wide.
She removed the front cover and the packing inside.
Stunned with pleasure she could not hide.
She bit her lip and stood there and cried.
Through the floods of tears her heart was throbbing.
She was alone in the world, inconsolably sobbing.
"Oh, Leon, I love you. Why have you not rang?
I prayed you would phone once my plane did land.
I am stricken with grief. My heart is in two.
Every one of these tears is cried for you.
If I knew then, what I now detect.
I was not thinking clearly and would never have left.
I'm so sorry, my love. Forgive me. Please do.
It's something I wish I had not put us both through.
I pray you still love me, and I've not made you sad.
Being with you are the best times I have had."
She felt like the woman with white wings who'd said goodbye.
Her mascara diluted by the tears from her eye.
Right at that moment her cell-phone rang.
An unrecognised number from a foreign land.
"Hello, hello. Is that you Leon?"
"It is, Monique. Sorry it took me so long.
I was not sure if it was OK to disturb your writing.
But being away from you has been almost frightening.
I bought a one-way ticket at the airport in Milan.
The destination on it, says Amsterdam.
Do not leave the house for I will come and find you.
We can stand at your top window and take in the view."
The door knocked again. She thought, *Not now, please.*
The driver must have misplaced his keys.

"Hold on Leon. Just a second, my dear.
Your delivery driver has just been here."
The line got cut off as she was near the door.
But she had the number and would return his call.
She opened the door and didn't believe what she could see.
In a tuxedo, offering a ring, Leon was down on one knee.
"Monique, if I do not do this now, I'll be damned forever.
Will you marry me, my love, so we can always be together?"
She went into shock. Heavily palpitating.
She burst into tears as he knelt there waiting.
She was panting out, with every breath.
Staggered intakes. Hair stood on her neck.
She cupped her hands over her nose and mouth.
Black streaks down her cheeks had her look like a clown.
She made whimpering noises. She physically shook.
She felt like being in the middle of a love storybook.
She fell to her knees, taking handfuls of her dress.
Through her breathlessness, she uttered the word "Yes."
Her face was contorted but with a hint of a smile.
This leapfrogged imagination by a country mile.
She fell into his arms. He held her gently.
A vision of love for anyone passing, presently.
"Monique, please stand up. This has to be right.
I will only do this once in my entire life."
She got to her feet. He held her left hand.
For, after this moment, all else was unplanned.
"I have dreamed of you every single night.
Your face in my mind like an angel in flight.
When I wake you're there throughout my day.
Warming my soul like a sunshine ray.
My streak of love is a mile wide.

I will be forever happy if you would be my bride."
He felt like a prince who was about to be king,
As he sealed their love with a fat, diamond ring.
It was a perfect fit. He'd taken one hell of a chance.
In an age-old fashion of true romance.
He stood up and they kissed. Her pleasure replaced pain,
As all the electric returned again.
She brushed her hands all through his hair.
Kissing him non-stop as she still gasped for air.
She withdrew from his lips. She had to look at her ring.
Being so loved was a beautiful thing.
The sun caught a facet. It sparkled in her eyes.
She felt her whole world as she looked at blue skies.
She took his hand and led him inside.
Her uncontained joy was in override.
Real lavender sat proudly in an ornate pot.
Its unique aroma covering every spot.
Side-by-side they walked up the stairs.
Taking each other in with long, loving glares.
Four flights seemed like nothing as they passed through the
door.
A twenty-paned window almost spanned the wall.
The long, looping arch that ran over its top,
Framed Amsterdam perfectly as its lively backdrop.
They stood. They said nothing. They just took in the sight.
Both turned on to the idea of afternoon delight.
"Would you like to see my bedroom?" Monique said.
He replied, "That very thought just entered my head."
They moved to the next room. She opened the door.
A king-size, four-poster dominated the floor.
Leon raised his eyebrows and had a little laugh.

"Well Monique, we could have some fun in that!"
She turned to him and pulled off his bow-tie,
Made a kissing gesture then winked her eye.
She made it taught as it was in her hold,
Then placed it on his eyes to make a blindfold.
Straight away his heart accelerated in pace.
He felt her warm breath close to his face.
She kissed his lips and quickly retracted.
He kissed fresh air by the time he reacted.
She brushed his chest. Gripped his shirt with both hands.
Then ripped it open. Buttons flew off cotton strands.
He reached out to touch her. She knocked his hands away.
She was in control. She dictated their play.
He started to speak. She shushed him quick,
By placing two fingers onto his lips.
She took his shoes and socks off then stood behind him.
Leon was excited and shaking as he held a forced grin.
She removed his jacket and placed it on a chair.
His growing anticipation was not her care.
She grabbed his shirt-collar and pulled it right down.
So it hung from his wrists, inside out.
She kept a hold and began twisting it round.
To the point where his hands were tightly bound.
She undid his pants. To his feet they just fell.
She knelt in front of him and pulled his shorts down as well.
He felt completely vulnerable. Unable to break free.
She said, "Do not worry my darling. It is only me."
Her words relaxed him, so he let go of his defences.
As, in these moments, he was deprived of some senses.
She was stroking his legs and kissing his skin.
Her cheek brushed his thigh to keep contact with him.

She reached round for his shirt and started taking it off.
He ripped it in two like tearing a cloth.
She dropped off her dress for more moments to share.
As she stood up in her white, lace underwear.
He removed the blindfold away from his eyes.
He thought she was the most beautiful woman alive.
She was stood with her hands behind her head.
Leaning against one of the posts of the bed.
"Stay there," she said. "I have a little treat."
She slipped a pair of stilettos onto her feet.
With each finger and thumb she pinched the border of lace.
To check her stockings were in the right place.
She picked up a remote and began to sway.
The sound of slow music started to play.
She turned around and put one finger to her lips.
Then walked over, as models do on catwalk strips.
She placed a hand on his shoulder and dragged it over his chest.
As she swept behind him he felt the touch of her breast.
They stood back-to-back. He could feel her cool cheeks.
It was a divine example of how energy speaks.
A photographer would die happy to capture this in motion.
It was the purest product of human emotion.
She moved her head from shoulder to shoulder.
His back arched inward. He was aching to hold her.
She spun around with one shift of her feet.
With her ear to his back she could feel his heartbeat.
The music grew louder with a fast, flute-like, sound.
Her heart skipped quicker and began to pound.
She moved around him like an Egyptian dancer.
Excited with the feeling of being this true romancer.

She danced to the music as if performing to an arena.
Like a routine that had been choreographed for a ballerina.
On her hands and knees, she moved in a cat-like fashion.
With all the animation of a Chinese dragon.
As the music reached its dramatic peak.
She slumped to the floor and lay at his feet.
His mind took snapshots for permanent proof.
As she lay, making poses, as if it were a photo shoot.
He knelt down on the floor. Placed one hand on her leg.
She smiled with her eyes closed as she rolled back her head.
Her arms lay flat as though she were reaching up high.
His hand slid slowly to the top of her thigh.
She kicked off her shoes and placed her soles on his knees.
Then said, "Drive me crazy and tease me please."
He grabbed her waist and moved up her ribs.
She pushed out her breasts and stretched her fingertips.
He caught the outline of her heaven between her legs.
Every muscle in his body became instantly tense.
He passed over her skin. She was almost in fits.
He had her pinned with his weight by her slim, little wrists.
His love rubbed at her underwear again and again.
She was overcome with an excitement that scattered her
brain.
He was forcing himself in her. His pain, more than mild.
The fact he could not enter drove her totally wild.
He released his grip and moved down her arms.
With each index finger, he unhooked her bra.
Then he pulled her panties halfway down her legs.
Held the back of her knees as if her cupping her breasts.
He sat back on his heels and slid his love down.
Then entered her deeply, which made her frown.

Her eyes were closed. Her lips pushed out.
She drew air through clenched teeth and let out a shout.
Her feet now sat upon his chest.
He placed his hands on her knees and pushed them to her breasts.
Then he closed them together. She put one foot on his face.
Biting the sole as he quickened in pace.
Her feeling-sensation was instantly raised.
Her eyeballs white, looked sexually crazed.
He grabbed her ankles. Both her feet covered his eyes.
She lay in pleasure, opening and closing her thighs.
With both her hands, she pulled forward her head.
The muscles in her stomach were completely tense.
Blind again, he reached out to fresh air.
Like being in pitch-black and hoping to find something there.
Their arms locked together. She could see him grin.
A pleasurable pain as she dug her nails in.
Deeper she dug till he could stand it no more.
He let out a shout with an open jaw.
This was sexual pleasure running through his veins.
A human moment that can rise above pains.
She let go of her grip. Took her feet from his face.
He ripped clean through her bra and held two pieces of lace.
She was beginning to moan. She grabbed the post of the bed.
He was about to do something to push her over the edge.
He parted her legs. She gave an almighty scream.
As he plunged his tongue where his love had been.
It totally had the desired effect.
The timing of his action was completely perfect.
"MY GOD!!" she screamed, as her whole body exploded.
Joy exceeded reckoning as her juices unloaded.

Her pleasure brought him happiness as he carried on.
The sensation between her legs was like a shattering bomb.
He quickly sat up to rest on his shins.
The second shock was about to begin.
Bolts of orgasm rendered her into submission.
As again, he resumed his earlier position.
She had no idea which way to think.
Her jaw shook rapidly as she took air in.
He hugged her legs as if he were holding her body.
Her ankles clamped his neck, somewhat, forcefully.
Then she crossed her feet behind his head.
Drew him to her as his pelvis sped.
Deeply, they looked into each other's eyes.
This could have been a beach in paradise.
His expression became twisted. She felt a huge wave coming.
His pulse boomed in his head like tribal drumming.
Their gaze was fixed. Two souls were now locked.
Almost beyond belief as their world was rocked.
It was so explosive, Monique physically wept.
Like she had awoken in Eden, but having never slept.
She was at the very centre of a firework dreamland.
Rockets of pleasure shot to her feet and hands.
Her arms and legs just fell to the floor.
He lay on her and held her as he could give no more.
They rolled over as she just wanted to lie on him.
The softness of her hair, brushing his skin.
She bobbed her head back and forth.
Kissing him each time as he rested on the floor.
He stroked his hands round her shoulder blades.
Criss-crossed down her back like a threaded shoelace.
They both felt so full and gratified,

With that feeling of being sexually satisfied.

She started to laugh. Just a little at first.

Quickly her chuckle became more of a burst.

She said, "I can hardly believe my overwhelming content.

Your master-plan spanned half a continent.

All that business of making me believe you were in Milan.

And you were already here in Amsterdam."

He said, "I just wanted to do something to leave you startled.

So I tracked that package once it was parcelled.

I was stood over the road when the drivers arrived.

And, looking right at you, I could see you were surprised.

Seeing you again made me convincingly certain.

For me, in this world, there is only one person.

The drivers left and I crossed the road to your house.

I delayed no longer and I had cast off all doubts.

I knew what I was doing was a little bit deceiving.

But my intentions were good. The idea was so appealing."

She ran the nail of her finger across her bottom teeth.

Still partially in a state of disbelief.

Then with one finger, so softly, round his features she was moving.

He closed his eyes as the feeling was so soothing.

In a circular motion she drew round his lips.

Then lowered her face and they began to kiss.

So much for them both from this most simple exchange.

How a beautiful kiss can take one to another place.

The giving of love and the passion for another.

Where much is discovered from kissing a lover.

Their eyes were closed. It seemed never-ending.

The joy of such love was completely mind-bending.

She said, "Shall we get in the four-poster? I've just put on

fresh bedding.
We can laze for the day and discuss a wedding."

Chapter 7

The next morning, they ate breakfast on the second floor.
Monique said, "Give me a minute," as she slipped out the
door.
When she came back in, she said, "Now close your eyes."
She was holding something that she was trying to disguise.
He played along and put his hands over his face.
Something had been placed at the side of his plate.
"Can I look?" he enquired. "Please do," she said.
He opened his eyes and looked to his left.
A red ribbon was tied on what looked like a gift.
But it was actually securing a manuscript.
He undid the bow and there in black on white.
Were three words of a play called At First Sight.
"Shall I read this now?" he asked, with a smile.
"Yes," she said. "I'll leave you alone for a while."
He turned the first sheet and began to read.
Moving through lines at a leisurely speed.
Very soon he could see a striking similarity.
A resemblance of feelings that had pleasant familiarity.
It was set far away with folk in summertime regalia.
Near the golden beaches on the coasts of Australia.
It was very descriptive of each person's action.

Such depth and magnetism of the main characters' attraction.

It was like a God and a Goddess were powerfully converging,

As the sweetest love was constantly emerging.

As it stole his mind, he was taken away.

He thought this could be a film, not only a play.

Pausing for a moment to scan the scenes in his head,

He had that thousand-yard stare from what he'd just read.

He carried on reading and was drawn further in.

To a world of love that saturated him.

Veronica and Marco were the leading roles.

Nothing could be more perfect for these two drifting souls.

She was tall and beautiful with gold hair down her back.

With that down-under vitality that would shine through any crack.

She danced on life's stage with childish light-heartedness.

Taking nothing too serious. Her smile always brought calmness.

A dancer, by trade. Her success hard earned.

Almost giving up as there seemed closed doors where she turned.

But she kept sweating it out at many audition halls.

Seeing the same faces as though they were all on tour.

When her break came it was right out of the blue.

At the point where her heart was giving up its pursuit.

She was in her local practice hall. Close to tears.

Beginning to realise her deepest fears.

A few drops fell from her loving, blue eyes.

She was at the end of a road that covered many miles.

She picked out a piece from a famous musical.

The sounds and the words, to her, were beautiful.

A message of love sent to everyone.

From the gorgeous Argentinean called Eva Perón.
Veronica closed her eyes and let it all go,
As the music crept through her with a calming flow.
She let every sound penetrate her being.
For the first time in her life her dancing found feeling.
Her moves were dramatic. Catching each note with precision.
Subtle, when they needed to be, without a hint of indecision.
The well of doubt now felt less enormous.
But she had a cutting feeling that this was her final
performance.
She was crying out her sadness and sheer desperation.
Though her life was about to see a complete transformation.
The music stopped. She heard the sound of applause.
A man and two women were stood by the doors.
He spoke first as she wiped away tears.
"That is the best performance I have seen in years."
She said, "It could be my last. I am about ready to give up.
I have chased my dream. Now I have a dry cup."
He said, "The metaphorical cup is never empty.
Its contents may change but there is always plenty.
If I had a full glass of water and poured it away.
There would be nothing in it, most people would say.
Yet, if we examined it closer with a little more care.
We would observe the fact, it overflowed with air.
The content of your cup is by no means spent.
I have a suggestion I would like to present.
Would you join the three of us for dinner at the restaurant
over the way?
You might be very interested in what I have to say."
They looked at each other. A feeling ran through them both.
Fusion had taken place that filled them with hope.

The two women were smiling and nodding their heads.
She felt whatever it was would leave her impressed.
"OK," she replied. "Let me get showered and changed.
I'll meet you over there. You can get a table arranged."
The two women left. Leaving them alone.
It was then that she realised her feelings had grown.
He said, "Can you add your name to your magnificent essence?
My name is Marco. I am humbled in your presence."
She said, "You're very charming. I like your no-nonsense style.
I am Veronica," she said, with a smile.
"A perfect name for a perfect face."
Then he muttered, "Could this be the end of my incessant chase?"
"Pardon?" she said. "Oh nothing," he replied.
Then his whole demeanour became more amplified.
"Well then, Veronica. I hope to see you in an hour.
I will leave you be, so you can get a shower.
Just one thing that I must tell you, albeit, so soon.
Immovable attractions lead me right to this room."
A frozen moment swept over them. The world's clocks all stopped.
Her arms relaxed at her side. Her shoulders dropped.
He placed his palm on her cheek and brushed his thumb under her eye.
The moment hung forever in timeless time.
His hand pushed her hair behind her ear.
As, very slowly, he drew her near.
They both closed their eyes. Their lips joined like two bubbles.

As a gift from life blew away any of their troubles.
His arm slipped round her waist. His hold became tighter.
She gushed with a feeling that made her feel lighter.
Her arms wrapped round his neck. She coiled one leg around.
Draped upon him like a white Roman gown.
A creaking floorboard, underfoot, made them jump in surprise.
They smiled as they stared into each other's eyes.
As he withdrew his hands, she could feel them shake.
He turned and was gone as the door swung in his wake.
Her head tilted forward as she looked to one side.
She had a startled look, but it was coupled with a smile.
He had taken her heart within a very brief moment.
She became an advocate of love or, at least, its newest component.
She floated away to get washed and changed.
All her feelings had been rearranged.
If she looked a million dollars in the studio you could now times that by fifty.
Her presence in the restaurant had eyes shifting quickly.
Her eyes met with Marco's. His face was enthused.
He stood and beckoned her to take a seat in their booth.
"Please sit next to me. What would you like to drink?"
"Water, for now, please." As, into the seat, she did sink.
He said, "I will not waste a second for timing is crucial.
I believe our coming together will be exceedingly fruitful."
Veronica looked at the two ladies. They were as excited as him.
Something especially wonderful was about to begin.
"Well, out with it," she said. "Delay no more.
Give me the news that you invited me here for."

"Oh Veronica." He sighed, as he rubbed his brow.
"I knew if I kept looking, I would find you somehow.
I am a musical director who was, earlier, knocked off his perch.
I knew when I saw you, I had ended my search.
A script has been written. It was handed to me.
I've been granted free licence to set it free.
I could not be more excited to have been asked to do this work.
Though, looking for the right beauty has almost driven me berserk.
Then there you were as we walked through the doors.
Moving to that music. Making it yours.
How is your voice? Can you hit all the notes clean?
If you can, I need pinching as this may be a dream."
She looked at them all with one swooping glance.
Nodded her head as she meshed her hands.
She rolled her thumbs as she thought, *Yes or no?*
Without a moment's hesitation she decided to let go.
She placed her hands on the table and pushed herself up.
Took a small sip of water then set down her cup.
She walked away and stood at the front of the room.
Hummed a note so she could get in tune.
All the flickering looks now became obvious stares.
Marco and the two ladies sat at the edge of their chairs.
Even the waiters and bar staff all stopped what they were doing.
Everyone present thought this would be something worth viewing.
She cleared her mind. It was as if she were auditioning.
And right there in the restaurant she began to sing.

It was the song that she'd danced to earlier that evening.

Marco's mouth was agape. He was almost disbelieving.

Without the accompaniment of music, it was a magical sound.

He knew the star of the show had now been found.

But not only that, as there was so much more.

She was a beautiful woman who he would worship and adore.

As she hit every note, confidence dismissed all her fears.

Without a single flinch she had two wet lines of tears.

Whether she sang this song or heard it play,

It took her back to her earlier day.

Her eyes were shut. Her head angled back.

Every person in the room began to loudly clap.

People were cheering. A few cried out, "More!"

She showed her palms and nodded, then left the floor.

She had lit the place up and raised the atmosphere.

Staff were rushed off their feet for orders of wine and beer.

Everyone buzzed. Conversations grew louder.

As she soaked it up, she could not have felt prouder.

Marco was breathless when she retook her seat.

His clenched fist was placed between his teeth.

He almost dare not look at her as he said, "That's it.

Can we say nothing for a moment please, and just simply sit?"

They all sat in silence as he could still hear her voice.

He was brimming with happiness that she held such poise.

"Veronica," he said. "That was beyond all I could dream.

I am so thankful I have met you. Now picture this scene.

You'll be the diamond in the crown on the opening night.

In a story that's all about love at first sight.

We shall travel the country and you can sing and dance.

And unleash this tale of perfect romance.

You'll be a queen of the stage. A smash-hit sensation.

We'll put your face on every poster. You'll be adored by a
nation.

Then we'll take it to Europe. They'll love it to bits.

As each audience will demand encores for you to belt out
more hits.

You will taste the good life as everyone should.

I really could not make myself more understood.

These two ladies who are with me are my dance
choreographers.

As you can see by their smiles, they would love you to be part
of this.

You can put down your life and all that you own.

Travel and the stage can become your new home.

We have seen how you move. We already know you are
gifted.

You now have a choice and your whole life could be shifted."

Veronica's mind exploded with many pictures of her life.

Memories of her efforts. All the toil and strife.

She saw herself as a child at her first ballet lesson.

This was to be the beginning of a lifetime's obsession.

All those times she'd given everything and heard the word
"Next!"

As she walked away feeling broken and perplexed.

Never knowing she had only just missed out.

Crying in car-parks until comfort came about.

Picking herself up after every single fall.

Digging deep for the belief that it was worth it all.

Having never married as her career was her dream,

Years had slipped by her, almost barely unseen.

Now here she was at a defining juncture.

A decision had already, and quite easily, come to her.
She spent a few moments thinking about worth.
Then believed this was something life decided she deserved.
She looked at Marco and nodded her head.
"I want to experience every moment of what you've just said.
I've spent my life searching and striving for success.
In the end it found me when I felt under duress."
Then a compulsion took hold of her like never before.
She put her hands on his cheeks and knew she was sure.
"I think I'm in love with you. Will you kiss me again?
When we kissed back there, everything changed."
He looked into her eyes as love touched his heart.
Without a care for anything he took her in his arms.
In opposing booths men looked on in despair.
Wishing it was them who sat in Marco's chair.
There were women turned on and sat there glaring.
Wishing their lives had such understanding and caring.
The two dancers had been holding hands for some time.
They tightened their grip as their excitement did climb.
He pulled her close and felt her breasts touch his chest.
His hand slid up her back. On her neck it did rest.
He said. "I think I'm also in love. Which is something new.
I'd never had this feeling until I met you."
He kissed her with force. She was lost in the embrace.
A tear rolled down one of the dancers' faces.
She was witnessing love like she had never seen.
Completely taken in a waking dream.
Watching them kiss, right in those seconds,
Gave her the feeling this was sent from the heavens.
She thought, *Love at first sight really does exist.*
I am seeing it now. It must be bliss.

To know in one moment, it will hold you forever.
Guide you and lift you through any endeavour.
The two stopped kissing and let each other go.
Marco said, "Let's go and make one hell of a show."
They set off into the night. Their journey was far.
They kissed in the back seat of a prestigious car.
He talked of the story they were going to create.
A tale of pure love that was sewn by fate.
The lights on the highway whizzed by like white streams.
Veronica had been thrown into the middle of her dreams.
With someone to love, who offered the door to a career.
From her warm, leather seat she noticed daylight was here.
Marco was asleep. She admired his features.
It was a coming together of two beautiful creatures.
She was slipping away as her eyelids grew heavy.
Sleep took her in its arms as it knew she was ready.
When she woke, she had no clue as to where she was.
Still tired, as one gets when sleeping in cars.
The doors started opening. They all began moving.
Veronica used the smoked window to do some temporary,
light grooming.
She tried to look more official as though there was someone
to impress.
Marco put his hands on her shoulders, clearly seeing her mild
stress.
"Veronica, stop. You look perfectly fine.
Please relax. What you are looking at is mine."
He kissed her. Then held her and laughed once, through his
nose.
Then they laughed together as a good feeling arose.
She said, "I didn't know what to think when I looked around.

I thought I was about to audition. My heart started to pound."

He said, "You auditioned last night. I've never seen such grace."

He was struggling to peel the smile off his face.

"Two years, we've been looking. Now it is done.

In so many ways I feel I have found the one.

You have the voice of angel. It could bring tears to my eyes.

I would float on a cloud as your sound filled the skies.

Seeing your face when I woke up just now.

Let me know I'm in love, without a single doubt."

He took her hand. They began to walk.

A sense of knowing as they continued to talk.

She was absorbing the surroundings. So much to see.

This was a marvellous place to be.

White walls with red bricks, framing windows and an archway.

Black scrolling set in railings in a fantastic array.

They walked through the arch which contained a small tunnel.

The warm air sped up as it passed through this funnel.

He let go of her hand and reached into his pocket.

When it emerged again he held a round, gold locket.

She linked his arm. Her head touched his side.

Instantly intrigued as to what was inside.

With his thumb, he flicked it open. She was a little confused.

It was completely empty, which left her awkwardly bemused.

The empty chamber gripped her, where the backing looked old.

The meaning, she felt, was about to be told.

"When I purchased this charm, I decided to make a pact.

I would reveal its proper meaning when my feelings were exact.
As you can see it sits empty like a handless glove.
I swore I would never fill it until I was completely in love.
Now I see the face that makes it complete.
It's right there in my palm. It is yours, my sweet."
He had the ageless look of an innocent small boy.
Her heart's doors opened and were flooded with joy.
They stepped out from the tunnel. The sun shut their eyes.
She placed her lips on his mouth. He was nicely surprised.
He felt the wetness of her tongue breach beyond his teeth.
He kissed her even more as further feelings were released.
They were holding each other. She pushed her midriff to his.
Powerfully turned on by this sensual kiss.
Flashes through her mind of seeing each other nude.
Making love on white sheets. Not the least bit prude.
She saw him lying on her. Kissing her passionately.
Consumed by love and sensitivity.
They kissed a little more as they stood on loose stone.
She could not believe he owned this beautiful home.
Her sight had adjusted to the brightness of the day.
Gardens hung gently as if in Babylon on display.
Leaves wrapped around trellis. They fluttered on the air.
Scents arose from beds that were pruned with great care.
She looked back through the tunnel and saw the car drive away.
They were all alone to enjoy the rest of the day.
They made love that night in the outside glass-house.
It seemed every star in the galaxy had come to play out.
For the next two weeks he revealed the story.
How each act would unfold in all its glory.

She learned all the songs and any words in between.
Playing out her role in every single scene.
It was absolute magic. This would make her a starlet.
She was to play the lead character whose name was Charlotte.

Chapter 8

Auditions were held for all the parts of the show.

A leading male was still needed to give it balance and flow.

Marco wanted an unknown. Someone he could transform.

So that not only one, but two stars would be born.

Anyone auditioning had to learn two of the songs.

There was one on that list that no one had yet taken on.

The days were all long. Many people were seen.

Marco was getting anxious and twitching in his seat.

Veronica put her arm round him and whispered in his ear.

"Patience my love. You said to find me took two years."

Then a young man walked on and stood in the light.

He was asked, "What will you sing?" He replied, "At First Sight."

Marco's slouching posture was immediately corrected.

The two dancers' spines became instantly erected.

Veronica sat up. Her heart, it prayed.

The young man approached the microphone as the piano played.

They all listened intently. What would this man bring?

Calm and composed he began to sing.

Their spirits all lifted within two lines of the song.

His confidence grew as he moved along.

Veronica's seat had flipped up. She entered the stage.
The man who was singing looked a similar age.
He sensed her nearing as he carried on.
It was the lead female's turn to sing in the song.
He sang the last word and took a step to the right.
Veronica moved in and stroked her hand on the mic.
She sung her piece. Then they sang together.
Their unified sound was beyond all measure.
It could leave you in tears as music sometimes does.
It was full to the top of professional love.
Marco said, "That's it. It's him. He's finally here.
Auditions are over. Someone please make that clear.
The dream is alive. It finally breathes.
This had to happen because we all believed.
Did you feel that connection between this man and my lady?
Our two stars are born without hint of a maybe.
Young man, that was brilliant. Tell me, what is your name?"
"Thank you, kind sir. I am called Shane."
"Well then Shane. I have this to say.
Will you join the ride and be a star in our play?"
"I will sir. I will. Thank you so much."
The two dancers embraced in an excited clutch.
Marco stood up and made his way down the aisle.
From start to finish he held the biggest smile.
He jumped up on the stage and shook hands with Shane.
Took long stares at them both. Then went on to say,
"I have a vision of what will be.
Veronica will be Charlotte. Our leading lady.
Shane, you'll be the lead male in this extravaganza.
You, my friend, will play the part of Alexander.
What has just been witnessed was magic in the making.

Sparks just flew from this impromptu undertaking.

Veronica knows I love improvisation.

We'll need that on the way if we're to be a sensation.

Shane, I am Marco. I am the director.

This will change your life, and I mean forever.

So, I ask you now. Is it a yes or a no?

Are you prepared to let the life you know go?"

Shane released one deep breath as his forearms shivered.

He was blown away from the words just delivered.

He said, "I've not acted for some time, but I can sing and dance.

Will that set me back or affect my chance?"

"Hell no!" Marco said. "This is a musical play.

It will all move with ease in a wonderful way.

You will be in a comfort-zone. I will help you feel well.

Though, in your heart, you must strive to excel.

I want the best of you. Every ounce of your passion.

They fall completely in-love. You two must make this happen."

The two dancers were now present and stood behind Shane.

The whole group was buzzing as they gathered on the stage.

"Marco, my answer is yes. Just tell me what to do.

I will do my very best for you."

"Fantastic!" Marco said. "Let's begin right away.

We will go to my house where you can read the whole play."

They arrived and he took Shane to a quiet place.

So they could speak one-on-one, face-to-face.

"Shane, it's took me years to be able to now say this to you.

I know in my heart we can make it come true.

The world's just about ready for a beautiful tale.

I can feel success on a very grand scale.

Here's a copy of the script. Please sit and digest.
I am certain it will command your deepest interest."
He looked at the front cover. Then picked it up at the seams.
His curiosity was sparked by the one word, "Dreams."
Shane opened it up and began to read along.
The comments Marco made were not far wrong.
"I dreamed a dream many years ago.
A face appeared that I did not know.
She took my hand and led me away.
Where we went is hard to say.
We sat by a river on the edge of night.
I had fallen in love, at first sight.
We lay on cool grass. I stroked her hair.
I was in a place where I had no care.
She held my soul with her gentle hands.
And flew it away to unfamiliar lands.
I brushed past stars of the purest white.
Sparkling like diamonds against the blackest night.
She spoke about love. How hers was for me.
Could my human soul have been more free?
We crossed dimensions in seconds, of uncountable years.
I had laughter, sadness, joy and tears.
We were in her world. My clothes were like hers.
I could barely look at her beauty without feeling disturbed.
She spoke again. I was sweetly shocked.
A new door in my soul was to be unlocked."
"Alexander, I am Charlotte. I mean you well.
I am in your dreams to make it easier to tell.
Try not to resist against the words you now hear.
Let them rush through your veins and abandon all fear.
A connection exists from your world to all others.

A coming together of Sisters and Brothers.
It happens in dreams, every night, when you sleep.
While your body lies inactive. Your mind starts to creep.
The dream you're now in will be the clearest you've had.
So, take joy from its outcome and try never to be sad.
You and I are linked across time and space.
For, I am just another part of the human race.
This may all be difficult to assimilate.
But we are eternally bound by love and fate.
I know this feels like you are now here.
And you are, on every level, except physical, my dear.
Countless lifetimes we've lived, and never quite met.
So close, yet so far, in the universal net.
We almost met in your life, five years ago.
Our eyes locked once as a lift-door closed.
A glimpse of love on that fateful day.
For, hours later, my life was taken away.
As I crossed over, every person I'd met was there before me.
Through the endless faces, yours was all I could see.
My true love was revealed. My heart was on fire.
It was love like no other that fulfilled all desire.
I've been in all your dreams for the past few years.
Night after night, love has had me in tears.
I could wait no more. I wanted you to know.
The feelings I have. I just had to show."
"This cannot be true. You must not be real.
What you're telling me now could drive me mad, I feel.
Charlotte, how would I be able to ever to look at another?
Now I have seen the face of my eternal lover."
She took my hand. We began to walk.
As we did, she continued to talk.

"It cannot be avoided. It's a universal sensation.
The way of all things. It touches every generation.
Souls have never been twinned from the same universe.
The complexity is insurmountable and extremely diverse.
Each life we have lived we've drawn closer together.
The next time you cross we'll be in-love forever.
Our souls' counter-point will finally be seen.
No more apart. No more a dream."
"We walked through a garden with black marble pillars.
Set on sandstone blocks, to accentuate their spirit.
Carved angels held instruments that I had never seen.
Breaths felt so real, despite this being a dream.
She looked in my eyes. I thought she was about to sing.
Her sound and her words were a wonderful thing."
"I longed to be loved in my life, but it was not meant to be.
Yet, all this time, it was looking for me.
It found me in a way that could never be imagined.
In perfect harmony that was effortlessly fashioned.
I have seen my true self. A thing I will never forget.
I have also seen yours. Though you have not yet.
Follow me, my love, into this tunnel of light.
Our time is right now. It's called eternal delight."
"I already knew what I had to do.
I followed, holding her hand, as I marvelled at the view.
We came to a cave. The brightness grew.
A spectacular unfolding of things I never knew.
I saw others for the first time. All beautiful girls.
Sat in each of their lap were glowing, white pearls.
They gestured with one hand for me to walk toward a pool.
It was the most magnificent, inviting, small blue lagoon.
Steps led me to its edge. The whole place was gleaming.

The walls of the cave appeared to be breathing.
I was encouraged to walk on. The water turned brighter.
Such a brilliant blue as my body felt lighter.
A sense of knowing took over. I stepped out with pure faith.
As I looked at my hands, I had become a wraith.
I stood on the water. It was healing my soul.
Never, could a human feel more whole.
Every second, the good feelings were more than doubling.
As I glanced down at my feet the water began bubbling.
There was magic here. It was running through me.
A presence in the water that I could not quite see.
Multicoloured swirls moving in figure-of-eights.
Leaving traces of their passing like a performer on ice-skates.
Becoming clearer and nearer. Rising all the while.
They surfaced from the water to meet my heartfelt smile.
A rectangular frame was climbing before me.
The excitement of the vision, we should all feel and see.
It held reflective glass that rippled like a lake.
The feeling was so real I was sure I was awake.
There was a crashing sound of a striking gong.
Then the sweetest voice began singing a song."
"Look deep into me and I will set you free.
I will turn you into what you were destined to be.
I am the forever mirror. My love holds no limit.
You are about to be shown your perfect spirit.
I will shift you into your most beautiful form.
In these coming moments you shall be reborn."
"The ripples stopped moving and all felt well.
I was completely taken under the deepest spell.
A reflection of myself walked towards me in the mirror.
I was a greater being. I was a peaceful figure.

Charlotte approached me over the beautiful blue.
Her reflection in the mirror was walking too.
We were standing on water. Two translucent souls.
The pure greatness of the universe and the beauty it holds.
Our reflections held the calm of a soft, summer cloud.
I had never seen myself appear so proud.
Our reflections placed palms on the liquid pane.
It was right at that moment everything would change.
Our reflections just smiled as they knew our thoughts.
We put our hands to theirs as adrenaline coursed.
Our reflections gave love. We were impossibly high.
A sensation of supremacy brought tears to my eye.
Our reflections began fading. They became very dim.
They were now wraiths as colour returned to our skin.
Our reflections turned round. Both began walking.
Disappearing into mist. We could hear them talking.
The full-coloured frame gently lowered down.
I looked to my left as Charlotte turned round.
And there she was for me to see.
Love had a positive hold of me.
She seemed more beautiful. I took a deep breath.
We walked to the edge and stood on the step.
All the girls with pearls swayed side-to-side.
Cross-legged, with their arms stretched. The most beautiful
smiles.
We smiled at them all. They carried us along.
In perfect unison they burst into song."
"Now you both see. Now you both know.
Now you're both part of the eternal flow.
You see each other. Your love flows like a river.
You have been given the gift from the forever mirror.

Take your love now. Take it away.
Take it beyond the stars every single day.
This will last forever. This day is yours.
This only happens once. We offer our applause.
Set yourselves free. Set sight on eternity.
Set your hearts' intention on ecstasy.
Be in-love forever. Be two souls who are free.
Be all the things you ever dreamed you could be.
Sail on free air. Sail without a care.
Sail before sunsets for you both to share.
Today you are made. Today you can play.
Today is the birth of all you wish to say.
Tomorrow, who cares? Tomorrow, who knows?
Tomorrow is the place where today's love flows."
"I kissed her lips. Sparks flew through my veins.
Something was different. Something had changed.
I was really holding her. I felt her warm breath.
If this is how it happens, I offer my soul to death.
The girls were sounding a tone. It was the purest note.
When we descended the steps, I was sure I could float.
At the entrance of the tunnel we merged with the day.
The sweetest, soft wind just blew by our way.
There were people in the garden that were not there before.
Each as perfect as the next. Such beautiful form.
I was intrigued by a group talking beneath a pergola.
Charlotte sensed my interest and led me over.
By far, the most beautiful creatures I had seen.
They buzzed with an excitement I could not believe.
We were welcomed by a man who looked like a god.
His ebony skin glowing as he gave us a nod."
"My friends please join us. This you must share.

A joyous day where we are to become more aware.
We are here today because the time is right.
We are to be honoured with a gift called next best sight.
We will go into the cave. There we will shimmer.
This day we shall walk through the forever mirror."
"They left and we watched. We were smiling together.
They left. We held hands. They were gone forever.
The brightest white light that could possibly be.
Burst from the cave for us all to see.
It affected everything, including my soul.
Like every instrument of an orchestra had lost control.
I felt like a child. I was so innocently touched.
It took my breath. My emotions were clutched.
Confusion took over. I strained to think straight.
I looked to her as though I carried the world's weight.
Charlotte, how can I touch you? Why does this feel so good?
What can you give to make this better understood?
She started to speak and in no time at all.
Everything became clearer as I slumped to the floor."
"Alexander, my darling. I knew it was coming to this.
Let me sit at your side and make clear any mist.
Such is the way of things. We all have this time.
The feeling you now have. I once had mine.
A sense of being lost. Detachment from what's real.
Every single person gets to feel how you now feel.
It must be so if our hearts are to let go.
The mind can then grasp the ease of the flow.
A moving on is the plan that's always been there.
Whether you are aware of it or not or even care to care.
Acceptance is the path you must now walk on.
As big as you feel. You know a part of you has gone.

But it is not lost. You have only gained.

This stage of the journey is never easily explained.

This is the beginning. Now you have no end.

The body you left tonight has now gone, my friend.

You are your higher self. You are that greater being.

You are expanded consciousness. You are now all-seeing.

You are an angel. You can visit all dreams.

The fabric of your life now has no seams.

You have grace beyond grace. You can dream new ways.

You can think a thought and it will appear in your days.

You have the vision. You have spiritual flight.

You have been blessed by the mirror with what we call first sight."

"Like a thrown stone in flight before it hits a still lake.

I was at a universal passing-point and I knew I was awake.

And as a stone hits the surface and plummets down.

The effect of its passing is felt all around.

A sensation burst from my heart and mind.

She drew a sharp breath at the very same time.

She felt my feelings. She felt their might.

Charlotte, please explain. What is first sight?"

"First sight is for you. First sight is for me.

First sight is the next level where we are set free.

First sight affects everything to do with your life.

First sight is the unfolding of your souls' next flight.

First sight is the paving of a brand-new path.

First sight makes sure that, every day, you will laugh.

First sight is pure love. First sight is unique.

First sight allows everyone to openly speak.

First sight lets us put worry aside forever.

First sight is our guide. First sight is so clever.

First sight reveals people we've yearned to meet.
First sight lays our dreams right at our feet.
First sight is an understanding that propels us forth.
First sight is the acknowledgment of the unseen force."

Chapter 9

"Come on. Let's go. I want to show you the place.
We only have tonight and half a day.
We'll see the usual sights and as much as we can.
For tomorrow we'll be in London, having left Amsterdam."
Leon was shell-shocked and barely registered her words.
Monique's imagination had shaken his world.
He closed his eyes and moved his head side-to-side.
He'd been to another dimension that heaved his pride.
"Monique, wait. Please wait. I need some moments first.
I am in awe and inspired by your beautiful words.
I could literally shed tears at where these people are.
They're in a place so near and yet so far.
Does this place exist in the hearts of us all?
Is this the heaven that most hope for?
Where in that mind were these creations born?
The innocence of pure love. May it never be torn.
There's so much I could say as to where I have been.
The pictures you have painted could be viewed in a dream.
How ironic is that statement, given the title of the play?
I can barely explain where you have taken me this day.
Come real close so I can sense your scent.
Let me embrace you wholly, to feel the warmth of your

breast."

She moved to his side. His arms made a loop.

He held her with the chemistry of a ladle carrying soup.

She poured upon him like Irish cream over ice.

He groaned a sigh as he peered through her eyes.

They were in-love, and it could not be translated into a form of word.

In-love, at the highest level, like the freest bird.

Love that holds you and has you laugh like a child.

The kind that shines in your face and gives you those wild eyes.

He just sat there and held her. His ear near to her heart.

She put one hand on his head and brushed his hair in a part.

She placed the nail of her index finger between her teeth.

Absorbing his expression before wanting to speak.

A smile appeared across her beautiful face.

An eased silence remained as her eyes became glazed.

He stood and took her gently by her silky-skinned hand.

Led her to the bedroom. He had something simple planned.

He unclothed her body and made himself bare.

Gestured her to the bed for her to wait for him there.

She lay on her side. Her palm supporting her head.

Her eyes were following him as he walked round the bed.

As he left her sight, she rolled onto her back.

He never said a word, which made her laugh.

He just held a wry smile and gave her a wink.

Giving nothing away, so she didn't know what to think.

He moved back round the bed, looking right in her eyes.

She smiled back as he then lay at her side.

He kissed her lips. So soft. So sleek.

Pulled her in close and continued to speak.

"I want to tell you about some of the thoughts I have had.
The visions. The dreams. Not one of them bad.
They came to me first when I was all alone.
I was taking a walk not far from my home.
They inspired that painting that sits downstairs.
And had me sitting quietly with blank, vacant stares.
My mind was like a camera just clicking away.
Seeing heavenly images as clear as day.
I saw radiant figures suspended in space.
When I focused on the visions, I could see your face.
This was a new beginning, unfamiliar to me.
I totalled the visions. It came to twenty-three.
You now have the first. I need another twenty-two.
Every single one of them is a vision of you.
I have a grand idea and I must know your thoughts.
Before I can pin them upon gallery walls.
I want a string of masterpieces, or classics, if you like.
To be showcased at a place in one clean strike.
It will take half a year and I will need you there.
To take in subtleties of your being, so as not to be impaired.
Many will come. Their desire will be great.
Others will arrive because they like what I paint.
When these images are seen they will think it a dream.
They will shake with emotion. They will know what they feel.
These paintings could travel to all corners of Earth.
A tribute to you that, in my mind, you deserve.
There is a theme to it all. I will give it a label.
A reflection of all the paintings. The Wingless Angel.
Many a starry night set upon the purest white.
Like portholes on a ship, when observed at first sight.
It will be so fantastic. A dream will live.

This, to the world, I must surely give.

Monique, I am not here for the town or a particular view.

Love brought me to see one thing. That one thing is you.

Your beautiful body could easily boil my blood.

Your simple smile could bring me to ground with a shattering thud.

Your blue eyes hold no disguise. They are like the deepest pools.

The black orbs at their centre are, surely, onyx jewels.

I could not compare your most beautiful lips.

To be kissed forever whilst stroking your hips.

Yes, I am here, and my love certainly yields.

I could take you and make love in orange, poppy fields.

But right now, my love, I need to just look at your face.

How could I ever not love you while I am part of this race?

Being in-love with you makes me want to laugh at the world.

You're the exact reflection of my perfect girl.

We are all made this way so that we may find our true love.

Else, life would close its eyes and we would never open up.

Like wild flowers in fields that show all that they are.

Or the flickering light of the most distant star.

I have fallen. I have fell into a wishing well.

It feels like a dream or a wizard's spell."

"Leon, how can you capture such imagination?

When you voice thoughts, they sound like a revelation.

My little life seems to grow in stature.

I hardly contain the overwhelming rapture.

I say we forget London tomorrow and just head for your home.

Explore love together and be all alone.

I've got six months to fall into the depths of passion.

Where we can embrace two seasons in a care-free fashion."
He ran his hand down her side and left it on her cheek.
Then gripped, tight and quick, which made her squeak.
"Good boy," she said. This turned him right on.
"Let's move a step further where all inhibitions are gone."
She took control and forced him onto his back.
Dug her nails in his chest in a savage attack.
She raked all ten slowly down to his groin.
He feared her scraping right through his loins.
"Good God Monique. What are you doing to me?
Are you determined, in this bed, to turn me into a freak?"
She said, "Quiet yourself. Do not speak a word.
Scream as much as you want. It will not be heard.
You are sexually mine, right now, in this space.
I can tell you. We're about to go to another place."
She was breathing sharp. Her nipples stood proud.
The vibration running through her held the force of a storm
cloud.
She was seeing the pictures that he had told her of.
Her eyes were closed as she became more turned on.
She straddled his knees. Nails back in his chest.
He felt the power of this second pain test.
This was slower and harder as he showed all his teeth.
His desperate anguish could clearly be seen.
Her body moved up his legs. She pressed hard on his
erection.
It tensed instantly against her warm, smooth complexion.
She opened her legs to feel the tip of his love.
Lowering herself slowly as he anxiously looked up.
Rolling her hips as she leaned closer in.
She held his wrists to the bed which excited him.

Her movements were shallow. He dare not thrust.
Submitting to her control. He gave all of his trust.
Tighter she gripped. His hands started to go numb.
He made two fists as she carried on.
She brought them together above his head.
Sunk her teeth into triceps. They almost bled.
Then she bit at his chest two or more times.
Licked tenderly and kissed passionately on the scratched, red lines.
Without hardly noticing she had took all that he had.
Her juices were flowing like an open tap.
She brought her knees up so they dug in his ribs.
Then placed her palms at the top of his hips.
With her shins on the bed she began to lean back.
Just a little, at first, so he did not want to retract.
Further she fell. The back of her head touched his feet.
The pain between his legs arched his back off the sheet.
He moaned out loud. It was long. It had feeling.
His eyes filled with water as he looked to the ceiling.
His body was T-shaped. His whole face became tight.
She began her movements. They were ever so slight.
Her understanding of what she was putting him through,
Was felt deep in her heart and she knew he knew.
The love she had for his acceptance of pain.
A deep-down sadism she could not contain.
A living force that took over her brain.
A reality that drove her sexually insane.
Now she began thrusting far more frantically.
Her pelvis moved with elasticity.
Her spine exposed its flexibility,
As her arms mirrored his in simple symmetry.

There was a buzzing in her ears. Her head became hot.
Every thrust touched her most sensitive spot.
He brought his hands slowly to her side.
Then rubbed his palms inside her thighs.
She reached down and placed her hands on his.
He flipped them over. They held each other's wrists.
She slowed herself down. The feeling was embracing.
They could feel each other's pulse. Both were racing.
In this beautiful moment Monique found herself smirking.
Sounds escaped. She made intentional jerking.
She let go of him. She had a devilish expression.
She clawed at her skin without an ounce of discretion.
With her upper arms she pushed her breasts to the sky.
The waves began rolling. She made a high-pitched sigh.
She wished, in her heart, for her pleasure to remain.
An everlasting moment was the thought in her brain.
The waves were now growing. Her body was shaking.
She was losing control as each one was breaking.
Her arms moved fiercely like shivering from cold.
Tension in her muscles that was uncontrolled.
Ever so surely, orgasms broke through.
And there was absolutely nothing she could do.
The whole of her insides were loaded with a humming.
Her skin tingled with excitement for what was coming.
Then a hung moment, like the cocked hammer of a gun.
Contained raging chaos, before kingdom come.
Like the menace of a hurricane. Creating its destruction.
Everything before it, offering no obstruction.
An, almost, electric belt that had never been bigger.
Bolted through her body as life pulled the trigger.
She sounded from her stomach. It vibrated through her

chest.

Former unspent energy made her feel she was blessed.

Then the full force was unleashed. She was kissing life.

She screamed at her universe with all her might.

It never stopped. The strikes carried on.

Like the full unloading of a twelve-gauge shotgun.

It had far more than she could want. Too much for one person.

Every breathing adult woman should feel this, she was certain.

It wrenched her stomach. Her legs clamped tight.

She ran her hands through her hair and pulled it tight.

Then she twisted each bunch as her palms felt her nails.

Two braids of hair that made perfect pigtails.

She kept on screaming. It was all she could do.

Involuntary spasms finding their way through.

It was untouchable glee for this beautiful girl.

She released her hair, which lay there twirled.

She placed her palms on the soles of his feet.

The softness of this union was a sensation, so sweet.

His toes tensed back. Tendons like a hard thread,

As she dug his nails in the back of her head.

Her body kept beating until it was almost numb.

Like two hands pounding the skin of a drum.

She held the expression of a person in pain.

So much sweat on her body. It looked like rain.

It had become exhausting. She just had to stop.

Sapped of energy. Her pelvis did drop.

For the first time in a while, she sat upright.

His back fell to the bed. She was a comforting sight.

She felt so special. She made wooing cries.

Every muscle felt stretched from her stomach to her thighs.
Now she would give, as she had been given so much.
These next moments required a most tender touch.
She slipped off his waist to lie at his side.
Brushed her cheek against the top of his thigh.
She ran her hand slowly, right up his leg.
When it reached the top, she lifted her head.
She shook her hair once, side-to-side.
To remove any strands that covered her eyes.
She looked at him with a wide-eyed stare.
He stroked the back of his hand over the top of her hair.
She took hold of him. Drew back on skin.
She rubbed his love either side of her chin.
Her gaze was unbroken. She made her lips wet.
She was to make an offering he would never forget.
He removed his sight as his eyelids closed.
So the feel of touch became more exposed.
In a long, slow movement she brought forth her head.
The gratitude from love waved right through the bed.
He placed his palms on his forehead. His neck rolled back.
More than he could have imagined from this loving act.
Moaning began from the depths within.
This most intimate pleasure she was giving to him.
Her pleasure from his pleasure was turning her on.
A step further was nearing. Another layer soon gone.
"I need to pleasure you too," he said, amid it all.
Her legs started moving towards the headboard.
She relaxed herself. She had rotated in a blink.
Her actions were quickening. She drew on instinct.
She felt no need to slow down. It was a sensual pace.
With her wide-open legs she offered herself to his face.

His response was slow, but it did not lack feeling.
Her body tensed randomly which had her almost kneeling.
His hands firmly on her cheeks, he kept her down.
He held a smile as she wore a frown.
His tongue and his lips were in automatic motion.
As his mind became distracted like he had taken a potion.
A growing feeling. He was taking shorter breaths.
Knowing in his heart there was not long left.
This was not just sex. This was love being made.
Complete giving where both parts are played.
Love with feeling, so they wanted to be there.
The kind that would have your soul floating in the air.
To be touched. To be loved. To be kissed. To be cared.
To be all the things your heart wants to have shared.
To hold another. To hold them true.
To submit to their love. To have them hold you.
All these things, they both accepted.
Boundless joy that was uncontested.
This most intimate compliment being paid to the other.
Why would anyone deny this their lover?
Leon grabbed his own wrist. He held her tighter.
Shaking began as his being became lighter.
He had to stop what he was doing. She carried on.
The speed of her actions had clearly moved on.
He felt it coming like a train on a track,
That speeds through a tunnel, penetrating the black.
His stomach muscles flexed. His legs tensed hard.
He moaned with joy. The experience was unmarred.
And just as a train explodes into light,
His love burst into the world in its unique flight.
He yelled as he held her. She pushed right into his face.

Life had chosen them to be in this perfect place.
His muscles gave way. The feeling was divine.
He crossed his arms round the base of her spine.
He held his loved one. He stroked her skin.
She meant absolutely everything to him.
The scene was of beauty. Of love and desire.
Reflecting his feelings which could not be higher.
She started shifting herself. He let her go.
She moved for his face. All sexy and slow.
"Oh, my love," she said. "That was something to take in.
If I could dissect what just happened, where would I begin?
That was so beautiful. I didn't know I was so pliable
And all the while you made me feel so desirable.
I hope my excitement did not hurt you too much.
I knew I was adding an aggressive touch.
I felt wild. I was mad. My sex was alive.
I just had to. Oh, look at these red lines."
With her head on his shoulder, she gently stroked his chest.
She kissed his skin. Put her leg on his legs.
"It was worth it," he said, as he was still catching air.
He put one hand on her back. The other on her hair.
No more needed to be added. He said just enough.
Her mind fell calm through the feeling of love.
With open fingers, he began stroking away.
She closed her eyes and began to sway.
She felt removed. She was in a flow.
Like listening to someone softly play a piano.
He was also elsewhere. They both were smiling.
It was mesmeric to be part of and if viewed, inspiring.
For him, these after-moments were just as special.
For her, these touches were equally exceptional.

They started to kiss. It was a calming joy.
Wanting to be bound by love's employ.
That appealing feeling when one's tongue touches a lover's.
Feeling what you feel yet, not knowing another's.
Giving all you can because the reward is lifting.
To accept all you are given as your senses are shifting.
That's where they were in this post-love scene.
Where unseen love makes all seem a dream.
She opened her eyes. Not a word was said.
They just lay, appreciating. Two lovers in bed.

Chapter 10

The key entered the lock. The door opened wide.

Outside warmth immediately filtered inside.

Curtains were slid apart. Blinds turned, allowing light.

A feeling on a face from warm sunlight.

The kettle was filled and flicked on at the switch.

A relaxing atmosphere that was pleasant and rich.

A hand was led to a large, darkened room.

The light cord was pulled. Not a moment too soon.

There were twenty-two easels. A canvas on each one.

Set out in a crescent, with rough sketches thereon.

He walked away and left her standing alone.

They were back in the place that Leon called home.

One echoing thud as her hand shut the door.

The sound of her heels moved across the wood floor.

Spotlights at all angles were perfectly positioned.

Depth in each piece that would be fantastic, once commissioned.

Some clothed. Some naked. Some standing. Some lying.

In one of the images the character looked like she was flying.

Monique's heart beat fast. It was an eerie situation.

She relaxed and remembered extending this invitation.

The details in the sketches were not all clear.

"Well, this is a pleasant surprise, my dear."

She started at the first. Moving left to right.

Expressions were unclear. Faces almost white.

She moved to the windows. Each had a black roller-blind.

Pulling bead cords. Each began to rewind.

She shifted to the door to turn off all the light.

So to be seen in an atmosphere, not so bright.

This time she stood back so her eyes could pick and choose.

It was only from this distance that they all began to fuse.

She got it. She could see it. It would be a sensation.

She was in-love with a legend and his imagination.

Deeper she went. To the point of closing her eyes.

From one to twenty-two, she thought, the name of the theme applies.

It was like looking at an old film reel when held against light.

Each picture merging. It was a brilliant sight.

She opened her eyes. She took in all as one.

Something picked at her mind. A thing that would not be gone.

Though they all stood out, one made her feel alive.

The figure adopted a swallow pose, as if performing a dive.

She stared at this. It said so much. Like a soul that could not wait.

And that soul had dived off life itself and gambled on the power of faith.

It said a thousand words. It inspired the spirit, with every part of its essence.

Like drawing breath when all goes your way and you swim in the grace of a presence.

Though it was still, it seemed to move. Black traces like a gymnast with streams.

She jumped rather hard, from an invisible swipe. Like taking a
wrong step in dreams.
There was a knock at the door. She blinked a few times.
"Come in," she said, as she made for the blinds.
Leon came in. He was holding two cups.
"Monique it's OK. Please don't close them up."
"Are you sure?" she replied. "The whole, light of day."
He said, "Right now, my interest is in what you have to say."
She moved back to him and accepted her drink.
Just before speaking, she took time to think.
"I am nervous about what is here on display.
Excited and happy. I mean nervous in a good way.
I want to strip naked right now, for you.
I am so turned on by what you can do."
He said, "Make yourself naked. I can start straight away.
I'll just get a palette and start mixing my paint.
He took their drinks. He put them right on the floor.
Then went to a room that he used as a store.
She pulled off her blouse and kicked free her heels.
Unbuttoned, unzipped and threw off her jeans.
She stood in her panties then thought, *What the hell!*
In what was clearly a split second, she removed them as well.
She threw back her head. Ran her fingers through her hair.
A beautiful woman without a single care.
Leon reappeared and stopped dead in his tracks.
He dropped his shoulders as his whole body relaxed.
Her eyes were closed. She seemed to radiate power.
The way she posed looked like she was taking a shower.
"Monique," he whispered. "Would you like to begin?"
With her eyes still closed, her face sported a grin.
"Where would you like me? Where shall I stand?"

He put his things down and took her hand.
They walked between sketches. There were four or five stairs.
A raised platform she'd not noticed that caught her unawares.
As they reached the top, he flicked a light switch.
There was a black, backless couch with a light-tan stitch.
"Lay here, my love. Lay on your left side."
He picked up a cushion made off soft, mock hide.
"I want you to relax and have your eyes closed.
I would like us to start with a really simple pose.
It may sound easy to begin with, but it will take a lot,
To stay in one place as I paint the plot."
"I will do my best. I've never done this before."
"You'll be just perfect," he said. "Of that, I'm sure.
Bring your knees to your chest and let your eyes rest.
This is a first for me so it will be a test."
He turned around and walked away.
He carefully began rearranging the array.
The easels were on wheels. He placed one close by.
At an angle where he could see her with a quick shift of the
eye.
She wasn't sure which had been selected.
He added intrigue by keeping the content protected.
She lay there trying to recall all she had seen.
Impossible to remember. The torment was extreme.
A black and white image began to pass through her mind.
Like a kite on a string being allowed to unwind.
Large at first. Growing smaller by the second.
With no time to define as inner urges beckoned.
Her mind began racing as she grabbed her shins tighter.
Feeling sure he'd produce something that would highly
delight her.

She thought of love. She appraised her stance.

Knowing, for its continuance, she would always give thanks.

She began to play a game, just there, in her mind.

A poem, giving thanks, where each two lines rhymed.

Thank you for today, as I have reason to smile.

I am in-love with a man who paints with style.

Thank you so much for the feelings I have.

That fill me. That lift me. That bring me to laugh.

Thank you for my body and what it does for me.

That I may lay here naked and feel so free.

Thank you, life. For letting me choose my thoughts.

So I can pick all the nice things from the infinite source.

Thank you for my mind that allows me to play.

And has me feel deserving that things will stay this way.

Thank you so much for giving love to me.

That I may offer the same, unconditionally.

Thank you to my universe in allowing me to create.

Transforming my adventures. Sewing new fate.

She was drifting off. Further away.

Words and feelings were starting to stray.

She slipped into sleep with that nose and mouth sound.

Leon stopped what he was doing and looked around.

He laughed a little. Finding it most amusing.

Clearly, he thought, *it's from all the energy you're using.*

He just sat and looked. Then wondered for a while.

As he was doing this she began to smile.

Right at that moment he knew he'd been chosen for his profession.

She completed the whole picture with this simple expression.

He took up a pencil and began sketching her face.

Course, at this stage, as it was more of a trace.

The timing was sublime. To see her smile amid sleep.
A special moment had been given. Something quite unique.
Time flicked by. She woke up sometime later.
Cool skin from lying still and a shiver to shake her.
"How are we doing?" she asked, with a laugh.
"We're good," he replied. "Shall I run you a bath?"
"Yes please. That would be nice."
Raising a smile. She didn't need asking twice.
He went to the bathroom and turned on the taps.
As he sat watching the water, his mind fell into a lapse.
A powerful waterfall, bouncing high to black sky.
A crystal figure breaking a rainbow was in his mind's eye.
Prisms bursting from her. A burning sun in space.
She screams in total ecstasy as tears roll down her face.
Flying through the stars from the explosion of water.
A pure symbol of freedom. He'd name it Universal Daughter.
The swallow-dive sketch was to be next on his list.
Her being there presently, left a chance not to be missed.
It was at this time he felt glad he was with her.
He was seeing the unfolding of the completed third picture.
She entered the bathroom and climbed straight in the tub.
He placed his hand on her shin and gave a gentle rub.
"Monique, I have a request. We could call it a whim.
As daft as this sounds. My love, can you swim?"
"I can indeed," she said. "Why do you ask?"
"I would love you to perform a simple task.
Can we go to the beach, right now, before you bathe?
There's a place I want to see you. It's at the mouth of a cave."
"Let's go," she said. "It sounds like the seed of something great.
I'll just pick out a bikini. You look like you cannot wait."

They got to the cave. He climbed quickly up the rocks. She followed closely, with the stealth of a fox.

They were stood quite high above a deep, incoming tide. He said, "Wait until I shout you, then do your best dive."

He dived. A crashing wave in the cave released a mighty roar. She stood on the rocks watching and thought, *You've done that before.*

He resurfaced and looked up, then shouted, "Monique, are you ready?"

She looked out to the sea. Then spread her arms to keep steady.

She was breathing deep. Nervous as hell. She could feel the sea air up her nose.

The excitement of what she was about to do was felt from her head to her toes.

Treading water, out of the way. His joy was clearly on show. He took a deep breath, opened his eyes and yelled from his lungs, "GO!!"

She left the rocks with an adrenaline rush. A heart that was running a race.

He was right in the place that he wanted to be. Looking right into her face.

She was totally focused as she cut through the air. Eyes lit with a blue, burning fire.

His face was a picture when he captured her look as if hearing a note of heaven's choir.

She hit the sea. He closed his eyes. He laughed and put his head back.

This could end up being his best. White crystal enhanced by black.

He was to be gifted twice more, though he did not know. He

was excited from what he had seen.

Waiting for his love to rise from the depths like the coming
of a mythical sea queen.

She broke the surface. Hair clear of her face. She blew water
off her lips.

Eyes closed, then open, he knew at that moment he'd just
seen the fourth and fifth.

"We have to go. We have to get to the house.

I must get what I've seen on the canvas right now."

Not questioning it for a moment. She swam to the shore.

No towel. No comforting. Just a head-down, brisk walk.

Back to the back-room. Palette, brushes and a mission.

There to be converted. A translation from a seen vision.

"Can I look at the second whilst you pencil your scenes?"

"Yes," he answered. "I hope it takes you to dreams."

The left-hand corner was her first point of call,

Wanting to see its name before it hung on a wall.

She read the words and there found worth.

An uplifting inscription. "Sister Earth."

It was beautiful in its expression. A marvellous title.

She closed her eyes and felt most delightful.

Sister Earth, she thought. *It says so much.*

As if she was embracing life and its gentle touch.

Where there is only you in the world and nothing else counts.

Alone, with feelings, and void of all doubts.

She opened her eyes and took one pace back.

Almost breathless with amazement at what was set against
black.

She saw her face once more. This second brilliant work.

Her shoulders bounced, from laughter within. All she could
do was smirk.

It saw her there, arms round legs, tightly curled.
Like a tattoo, covering her body, was a map of the world.
She stood alone naked, suspended in space.
With the most serene and understanding look on her face.
There were no other planets. There did not need to be.
She was all alone. She was Earth set free.
Monique's eyes filled with water. She was breathing through her nose.
To see herself so beautiful in this effortless, simple pose.
She turned to him. He brushed the picture with his thumb.
She was at the fringe of his vision, but he needed to get done.
He was almost there with the face of this piece.
Taking away sharp edges to make it neat.
Then he sat back and looked. He smiled, very pleased.
She felt this was a moment that had to be seized.
He looked at her. "That's the third one ready."
She moved to him. Very sure. Very steady.
He held out his hand. She took it. They kissed.
She sat on his knee as he dropped his things.
"You've been crying, my love. I trust you enjoyed the view?"
She nodded and smiled, then simply whispered, "Thank you."
He said, "As long as you understand Monique, this is something new for me.
I am hitting my creative heights in this unchartered territory.
It has opened a door that I am trying to walk through.
But the flood of ideas is keeping me from that room.
That's not a complaint. I am finding it inspiring.
At this stage of my journey, it's like all cylinders are firing.
So I need to ask you to give me one hour.
In order for this fourth image to totally flower."
"I understand," she said. "I'll refill the bath just now.

There will be some food prepared for when you come out."
He picked up his things and moved his chair,
As the face of the fourth stood there bare.
He began pencilling away. Two hours went by.
He stopped and thought about giving her some time.
They sat outside. There was no chat as they ate.
Leon stared blankly at his empty plate.
"Monique, I cannot sit here with you. My feelings will not
wait.
I dare not waste a second, for I need to paint."
"I know what you need, and I will leave you till you're done.
I'm going to take a walk, to watch the setting sun."
She turned away then looked back again.
He'd gone, with no time or need to explain.
Back to the third. Colours were flying through the air.
It was coming alive. He was painting with care.
Rainbows struck from palms and soles. Mouth, ears and eyes.
Nine prisms sent from the crystalline figure, from the earth to
the blackest skies.
A quick inscription at the bottom to name an amazing
creation.
Represented beautifully, he wrote "The Crystal
Constellation."
It was the middle of the night. He could wait no more.
He just felt compelled to paint number four.
A quick glance at the sketch with his palm over his mouth.
So now to transfer what was inside, out.
It took eight and a half hours of unbroken attention.
What was produced, again, was contrary to convention.
It was a circular face that held her looks.
Though, there were other features, this was the crux.

It was split down the centre. A face telling two tales.
Shadowed earth, against moon craters and scales.
Her eyes were closed as she was blowing out air.
As though she were exhaling all of humanity's care.
A slightly happy expression and a sense of release.
Such a magnificent look that held the promise of peace.
A fat sun, to the left, lighting the moon with its rays.
The whole picture oozed the feeling of summer sunshine days.
It was an eclipse. It was life. It was dark. It was light.
Something to be gazed upon as day crosses to night.
Where one could appreciate its message as the sun and moon share the skies.
A time when thankfulness engulfs for simply owning seeing eyes.
It was astounding and it circulated life energy.
This fourth wonderful happening, he called, "She is Chi."
Day arrived as quick as a light being flicked.
He was happy, so far, with the order he'd picked.
He needed a break. He had seen growth beyond belief.
Leaving the room slowly. He now needed sleep.
He woke up alone. He stretched and smiled.
She was singing in the background with the voice of a child.
He wandered through to meet her. Feeling fresh, once more.
He stopped to watch her watering plants as he leaned on the frame of the door.
She hadn't seen him. She carried on. She was lost in her own world of thought.
He folded his arms and coughed loud once which cut her absence short.
"Ah! Hello, my love. I know you were up all night. Anything

I can do for you?"

He nodded his head. Poured a coffee. Knowing he had more pages to flick through.

"Just the one thing Monique, which you could do." As he gave her a loving look.

"Right now, more than anything else, I could just continue reading your book."

Chapter 11

"As great as it felt, I could not help my shock.
Something had gone, that previously felt like a rock.
As I sat on the grass, I was realising fast.
Nothing that is, can ever last.
Charlotte, can you explain in simple terms.
The way or the workings of the universe?"
"Alexander. Let's sit and think. Consider a rose.
If observed, we could see where energy goes.
In winter it awaits the coming of spring.
For warmth and rain to change everything.
Then summer comes to set it free.
To unleash the potential of all it can be.
In autumn we see petals falling to ground.
A simple show of how things move round.
And winter returns to retake its seat.
As the four-season cycle becomes complete.
The plant is the house holding the secret of change.
For, never will we see the same rose again.
Even the shed petals become reborn.
In one way or another, they must change form.
Now let's look at your soul and try to unravel.
How does it shift? How does it travel?

It will always exist. It cannot, not be.
Always vibrating toward a new frequency.
A higher level of love. Now unseen from your life.
As usual, others will feel grief and strife.
But you know you are here. That means far more.
Springtime, if you like, where you begin to explore.
Petals emerging. A kind of repowering.
You and your universe are constantly flowering.
A residual of you will still exist from your life.
A mere shadow now. Just a part of a mind.
For, if a person can see you as a reflection in themselves.
Then that is the place where part of you dwells.
You could be labelled a memory though, this cannot be.
It's a way of interpreting what they can no longer see.
So, your life, the universe and all that you know,
Are accelerations of vibrations for you to learn or be shown.
So come with me, to the summer of your life.
Be the flowering rose in seasonal flight."
"It was now clear as day. A perfect explanation.
I was part of a new world. A brand-new nation.
My body was still. All that moved were my eyes.
More people appearing with peaceful smiles.
I looked at my hands. My magical skin.
That which was without was now within.
I glided my hands over tips of grass.
Feeling their life in one gentle pass.
A sensation, up my arm, as soft as a feather.
I realised all that is, actually lasts forever.
She had told something of me I had never considered.
My existence was forever. Eternity mirrored.
A million lifetimes to live. A new me in each one.

Soul circulation. More knowledge. More fun.

They may all exist now, and I had been given a glimmer.

If I was to believe what I had seen in the forever mirror.

A feeling took hold of me as a result of my thoughts.

Something was happening I had not known before.

I lay on the grass. The feeling charged every cell.

My shivering body felt exceptionally well.

I was breathing deeper. My eyes sat there lazing.

Whatever was to come, I felt, would be amazing.

I looked to one side and hardly believed what I could see.

From every direction, something was drawing to me.

Circular shadows on the ground. Each looked like a ring.

My eyes flicked to Charlotte who was happily smiling.

I could not move. A force held me in place.

I broke a smile as I looked at her face.

A whispering sound in my ears and also my mind.

All of existence became perfectly timed.

The shadowed rings were penetrating my skin.

I knew they were causing the whispering.

As each one entered, the feeling was sublime.

As each one entered, I heard a sweet chime.

Faster. Quicker. There were more and more.

Thousands of shadows shifting on the floor.

The whispers said, "Yes," so many times.

Like a pumping steam-engine with this song of chimes.

Then they were slowing down. I heard a final ring.

Who could have known what these next moments would bring?

She put her hand on my heart. All was drawn to this.

As she asked me to release my inner bliss.

I breathed a full chest of air and my heart was ready.

She moved her hand away as I lay there steady.
My joy. My excitement. My happiness. My laughter.
The welling feeling would change everything, hereafter.
Like death and rebirth. A cycle to be complete.
Tears found my ears. Not the least bit discreet.
I moved my head forward. Hardly believing what I could see.
A clear ring of pure brilliance was emerging from me.
It rose from my chest. It was pure energy.
As clear as water. How could this be?
It grew bigger by the second. It began to spin.
A noise was produced. It was the sound of wind.
It climbed to the sky. A thousand feet high.
Spokes shot to its centre. It was a blur to the eye.
It now looked like a disc. I could see my reflection.
What was the meaning of this soul projection?
I heard a voice. It kept saying, "Yes."
I felt my whole spirit was about to undress.
There came a murmur. It was a rumbling sound.
Sent from the skies. It was felt through the ground.
I breathed a deep breath that could not be exhaled.
What, next secret, would be unveiled?
A shaft from the disc burst straight through my heart.
I screamed, euphorically, as all my air did depart.
I let out the last, to the sound of a blast.
Charlotte fell back and loudly gasped.
The disc opened in two, so similar to a locket.
Then it shattered into oblivion like an exploding rocket.
It covered the skies. I was breathing huge sighs.
Laughter consumed me as I rolled onto my side.
Then raindrops were falling like heavenly tears.
Clinking crystals was the sound that filled both my ears.

I lay there laughing. Drops touched my skin.
The experience of what happened was such a thing to take in.
I looked at her. She held an astonished expression.
Her hand on her brow. I felt it worth a mention.
Charlotte, you look troubled, my love. Is everything OK?
Is there something you want or need to say?"
"If you knew, you would not ask. You would have no need.
Look at their faces. See their love for what was freed.
In the years I have lived here I've never felt such a force.
In one way or another you are more connected to life's
source.
Let me look in your eyes, that I may sample a grain,
Of the love from your heart that governs your brain.
I thought I knew love and I did, in some way.
But I have just seen love created on this special day.
As we already know, love brings all things to pass.
With it, we are more. We become a greater mass."
"Our gaze broke off and we were both surprised.
People gathered round us with love in their eyes.
We got to our feet. I did not know what to do.
No sooner had I thought this, my voice echoed through.
What you have just seen was love supreme.
It was the heart of love. This is no dream.
For, I am you and you are me.
And we are leaves that live in the trees.
Greatness is yours if you can but believe.
Whatever exists is only what you perceive.
All that you know is a mirror of your mind.
All that you are is energy aligned.
All that you want your heart can bring forth.
All that you live is part of a force.

All that you can be, only you can set free.

All that you do, you do for eternity.

Appreciate yourself. Appreciate your lover.

Appreciate your sister and also your brother.

Appreciate your soul. Appreciate your senses.

Appreciate the dissolving of all your defences.

Appreciate your life. Appreciate each day.

Appreciate every breath and all the words that you say.

You are life itself. You are the answer.

You are the music and the human dancer.

You are the earth. You are the sky.

You are the fountain that touches life.

You are the magic. You are one.

You are the resonance known as OM.

The look on their faces said so many words.

I was shell-shocked myself at the profundity of the verse.

I took Charlotte's hand. I smiled and stayed calm.

As we began to walk a lady put out her arm.

She stroked my back. I could feel what she knew.

Her eyes lit up as her love shone through.

People placed their hands on me as we moved amid the crowd.

They knew I had channelled an energy that, to them, was behind a shroud.

Energy was being drawn from me. I could feel it passing to them.

But the more they took, the more I give. I felt like a living stem.

I heard the words, "Thank you," so many times. My heart was overflowing.

Charlotte's hand grabbed me tighter as we drowned in a sense of knowing.

We moved away. She was excited. I felt I could do no wrong. From the edge of the buzzing of happy souls I heard the words, "Not long."

I locked eyes with the man who uttered the line. It lasted less than a second.

In that brief exchange of simple glances, I knew he believed what he'd reckoned.

He became lost in the crowd. Gone forever, yet leaving a deep impression.

The peace in his voice. The look on his face. A most calm and simple expression.

I looked back twice, just to check. Something inside had been stirred.

A flash of an image shot through my mind. The briefest of voices was heard.

"He's right. He's right," is what was said. I saw myself floating above ground.

I glanced at Charlotte. She wasn't looking. I felt my heart start to pound.

Then it was gone, as quick as it came. I returned to a calmer state.

A stone arch and a wall, I had not noticed. Charlotte led me through an open gate.

It closed behind us. Sealing us in. Quietness all around.

The light notes of a mandolin produced a heavenly sound.

It was a circular structure with four other doors. A symbol etched on each one.

I turned around. I was totally surprised. The door we came through had gone.

There was a tree in the middle, tall and slim. It swayed side-to-side with ease.

An exhaled breath. A rustling sound, as warm air caressed its leaves.

At the foot of the tree a woman sat. A stone table with two spare places.

She looked at us. Raised her head once. We had excitement all over our faces.

As soon as she spoke, I had a lump in my throat. I felt my face going red.

I tried to act as natural as I could. It was her voice I had heard in my head."

"My friends take seat. Sit with me. I have something I wish to present.

In a moment you will see four carvings here. Each representing an element."

"She spread her fingers on the table. Her gaze, way beyond the near.

She lifted them slightly. Then moved them apart. Symbols began to appear.

Air, Fire, Water, Earth. They were the symbols that sat on each door.

I had a feeling I knew what was to come. My desire was growing, all the more.

Her attention went to Charlotte. I looked. She was happy as could be.

She pointed to Fire. They nodded once. Then turned their attention to me.

I already knew what I was going to pick. It seemed important to me.

I moved my hand and tapped down once. In doing so, I set Air free."

"Charlotte, come with me. I'll take you through. This will not take long, my dear.

Alexander, in a short time, I'll be back for you so relax and wait right here."

"We were to be apart. The first time since we'd met. I smiled as they walked away.

A peculiar feeling, I will never forget. I felt there was something I ought to say.

They walked to the door. The symbol shone. The woman raised one hand.

The door disappeared and they were gone. Off to another land.

I sat there intrigued at what had passed. It seemed so brief and concise.

I moved to the ground. Leaned back on the tree. To unwind and close my eyes.

Wind blew up my body. It stroked at my face. All my muscles fell calm.

My head touched the bark. I heard a bird sing. I yawned to my open palm.

I had never had such a relaxing feeling. The world around me felt right.

I opened my eyes. Two clouds crossed paths. Dark grey over the purest white.

The sun lit them up. My body shivered. They moved at different speeds.

A simple thing that covered my soul and left me free of all needs.

I was completely gone. The scene touched my heart. I felt I could openly cry.

A moment found. Then a moment lost, with just one blink of

my eye.

I looked to my right. She was back again. Smiling and standing alone.

I got to my feet. She held out her hand. Like a loved one welcoming you home.

We took our time. We just held hands. Then we stood before the door.

She knew I was nervous. I drew a deep breath. Her hand rose, just as before.

We took two steps. I saw a green light. Around, there was blackness to see.

She seemed to glow. The light moved closer. Then it raced as it passed through me.

A flight of stairs, snaking up, appeared as I saw a green spark. I reached out my hand. I touched the wall. It was rugged and smelt of bark.

The steps were hard mud with a small log at each edge. Wet, against my bare feet.

An ivory rail. Dim light being cast. The smell of the air was sweet.

We started to climb. We never spoke. Expectations being thrown everywhere.

I was consumed in myself. Of what to expect. I turned. She was no longer there.

The stairs were narrowing. Cool wind gathering. Adrenaline had my heart racing.

The light grew brighter. I was nearing an entrance. I was unnerved yet carried on pacing.

I reached the top and was almost knocked back. Misted glass between me and the next stage.

I heard sounds echo. I could see shapes moving. I yearned to turn the page.

Then right out of nowhere. Her voice in my ear. Clear and guiding me on."

"Close your eyes for the briefest time and the barrier will then be gone."

"I did as she'd asked. I looked down at my feet. There was one more step to take.

A shimmering stair, I would surely fall through. This was a leap of faith.

I paused for a moment to gather my courage. I forced my left leg in front.

Then I brought my right to stand in line. My body jerked from a shunt.

I disappeared into thin air. My breath became the wind. My soul had shifted into another form. Mind, just comprehending.

I had no feet to touch the earth. I moved through the feathers of birds.

I wanted to speak but when I tried, I simply could not form words.

I was above the clouds. I began to see stars. The edge of existence seemed near.

I felt myself thinning. Moving slower. I was skimming the stratosphere.

As thin as paper. A kite with no strings. Abandoned of feeling or care.

An impossible sensation with limitless measure. I had become the element, Air.

I spread myself and dived to earth. My being was a hundred miles wide.

With a whoosh, I flew just above ground. Nothing and no

one could hide.

I entered the lungs of a beautiful girl. She felt my life up her spine.

I knew she knew that she was being touched, by a force that was supremely divine.

I gauged her love from the middle of her heart. It beat like a living drum.

My cells touched hers. She stretched her arms. If she only knew what was to come.

I gathered air and drew it to her. She felt something she'd not known before.

I released all my love, deep from my heart. As this happened, she fell to the floor.

I floated above her, watching her face. The smile she held looked wild.

Then laughter erupted from the pit of her stomach. She was just like an innocent child.

I moved away. Floating off. An impression had been left upon me.

When I breathed again, I was sat with Charlotte. At the table, beneath the tree."

"Hello my love. You're here again. Try quickly to settle yourself down.

Being an element can upend one's senses. All that shifting and moving around.

Give me your hands and close your eyes. Relax. Let me speak in your ear.

There are a few things I wish to say while there is only you and I here.

The feeling you had in the lungs of that girl is almost beyond what words can say.

It always involves the heart of another, so the feeling is as clear as day.

You let your love go so you could fill her heart. Giving from the core of your soul.

You felt what she felt. She hit the ground. You could not have been more whole.

This may sound strange, but it is only the truth. In no way, do I wish to deter.

What you felt about the love you projected was not from you, but from her.

She is Air. She is the wind. She sent you high to fly.

She holds life in every breath from the earth to the endless sky.

You will always remember what happened today. It will hold you if times seem unfair.

As quick as a heartbeat. As close as a breath. You will never forget you were Air.

I want to talk about happiness. Inner peace and how best to keep things in tune.

At the heart of thinking there is a place in your mind. The door to another room.

I have already told you what first sight is. I spoke briefly of the infinite source.

Now I will tell you how it is harnessed and the way to plot every course.

Empty your mind of as much as you can. Allow the pictures to all go.

Clarity and transparency are what you must now let flow.

Take the first thing that comes to your mind. Feel it as if it were there.

Focus intently on its very existence as though you own it, or it was something to share.

In doing this you are transmitting a future, which will tie itself to what you're creating.

It now exists in the infinite source and in some way, it is there for you waiting."

"The image I saw was simple and clear. I held it between finger and thumb.

I turned it round. I examined it closely until the tips of my fingers went numb.

I had it. I held it. It belonged to me. This moment would stay with me forever.

It was grey on its back. White underneath. I was holding the stem of a feather.

Set on the white was something confusing. A red spot I kept trying to erase.

My efforts were worthless. It just reappeared. Like the sun in the sky bringing days.

I accepted this truth. It was a beautiful image. It was absolutely shaped to perfection.

It was a dream in my mind. The soothing kind. An exquisite and colourful conception."

"Now let it go. Open your eyes. The universe will take things from here.

You've done your job. It's now down to time. It knows your vision was clear."

"We stood up together. The arched door was back. The whole experience was surreal.

I had grown on this day. In a special way. Things took on a different feel.

A seedling of knowledge was then born in my mind. A fragment of appreciation.

Charlotte moved away from me, as though sensing a new transformation.

This seed in my mind was as real as could be. A green shoot appeared from within.

I felt it growing inside my head. It got to my neck and my chin. It multiplied four times or more. Green veins could be seen on my face.

All through my body, a new life was running. Down my legs it began to trace.

I stood so tall. My arms spanned out. Then something amazing occurred.

I moved out of my body. A thousand aromas. The sounding of a single word.

I dropped to my knees. Then sat on my heels. In the end, I lay on my back.

Green stems grew down and touched the ground. Then pushed through every crack.

I kept hearing the word. A hundred men. Saying it like a ticking clock.

"Earth!...Earth!...Earth!...Earth!" As sure and as steady as a rock.

Then pictures were forming as they weaved this word. A new image each time it was spoken.

A history of Earth inside my mind. Like a tapestry, sewn and unbroken.

I was sinking deeper into the ground. My arms and legs were changing.

I was soil and shoots. Moisture and roots. Atoms all rearranging.

Pictures of worlds. Countless planets. Formed shortly after their birth.

The chant reminding me every second that each was a different Earth.

I felt the earth spin. We joined as one. Every breath was so full.

Fields and fields. Magnetic fields. I was between gravitational pull.

Then a female voice. One I had never heard. Speaking a beautiful rhyme.

Peace in her voice. Offering knowledge and choice. Old age and youth at the same time."

"Take me. Touch me. Feel me. Be me. Breathe my life-filled love.

I am Earth in ten million places. Unique like a page in a book.

My brothers and sisters are solar systems. Their names you already know.

Jupiter, Mercury, Venus and Mars. Others like Saturn and Pluto."

"Then the sound of explosions. Enormous collisions. Too loud for my hearing to take.

I was pinned by all limbs. Plates began shifting. I was to feel the force of a quake.

A feeling like no other sent forth a shudder. Smashing rocks up the cord of my spine.

I laughed at the world with unparalleled joy. I kissed bliss and could only smile.

Her voice returned. It had a different sound. I could sense her excitement was high.

My breathing shifted into deeper cycles. The rumbling began to rise."

"I am an organism and you are the same. Always striving for correction.

Like cells fighting bacterial foes. Searching for a balanced direction.

Our universe is a wave-filled ocean. Never-ending change.

Ripples through space at a magnificent pace, where nothing is out of range.

I can feel the feelings deep in your heart. I sense that you are a little scared.

Your fear will serve you in the moments to come, as this will never be equalled or compared.

We coexist in the realms of space. You are forever linked to me.

I will leave you now, to another part of myself. I release you and set you free."

"The chanting stopped dead. There was total silence. I could only hear myself breathe.

My heart broke in two. I cried out loud, 'Oh God, help me please!'

My body began shaking. Pulsing and breaking. I was beginning to wish it a dream.

My stomach flexed. I felt thin and stretched like the bed of a trampoline.

She was right. I was scared. I moaned with fear. At one point I may have cried.

Horrific pain, that I could feel all over, making me wish I had already died.

It was in my head. It was in my mouth. Echoes too fast to split up.

It was like a freight train speeding or a woodpecker beating, to pierce a hole through wood.

I felt roots grow under every nail. They burst every finger and toe.

They wrapped my ankles. Bound my wrists. I thought they would never let go.

I screamed and screamed with all I had. It was unbearable beyond belief.

The force continued to pound my body. No mercy and no relief.

Then something happened, that had not before. My being became void of all pain.

My soul separated itself from me and I was functioning outside my brain.

I looked at my body. It didn't seem like me. My face full of peace and calm.

I knelt by my head. I thought I was dead, as I extended a comforting arm.

My hand touched my face. I stroked my skin. It was smooth like a piece of silk.

There was life in me though I was cold as could be. My skin the colour of milk.

I pitied myself. I was close to tears. I had the feeling of no self-worth.

Reminding me again as I sensed no pain, returned the chanting of "Earth!"

My wrists connected. Then my head. My soul pivoted round these points.

As though on a trapeze, I sailed with a breeze and felt life in all my joints.

I was reborn. Now having control. I took a firm charge of the quake.

I tensed all of my muscles. Roared from my gut. All heaven and earth did shake.

Here was a power that was beyond this world. It reached out

to places unseen.

I began to rise right out of the ground. My senses felt polished and clean.

With my hands reaching out, I stood there still. My heartbeat began to race.

Weak at the knees as I began to topple. I fell into Charlotte's embrace."

Chapter 12

"A place like this could well exist. There is part of me that would have it so.

You challenge my thoughts, my beliefs and desires. I can only dream what you know.

Your mind is amazing. What a gift you have. I cling to every word.

There are ideas here. Designs for living. Some of which, I've never heard.

The truth of existence. The belief in dreams. How we could be whatever we choose.

To treat others right for the rest of our life and we would surely never lose.

I love to love the simplest things. The sort we barely see.

Watching two people smile at each other and relating to how they feel.

A cloud in the sky just passing by. Silent, with its unmapped course.

Expanding or dissolving. It matters not. My mind rides it like a horse.

Walking slowly amongst all the people. Unnoticed by everyone.

Observing the pace of life through my eyes and feeling so far gone.

I like the feel of rain against my face and how it dances on the ground.

Or sitting indoors and closing my eyes and just drifting on its sound.

To lie by a fire with a non-stop stare. Hardly noticing what I can see.

Where all else around simply pales away and the world houses only me.

I wonder how many days I will live. How I could make each one of them good.

The odds of achieving goals set in life. New ways to be understood.

I like to slow life down by watching a clock. The seconds just ticking away.

It's amazing the time I can find in a minute. A chance to escape and play.

Or taking a moment to think of my heart. The effect it has on the world.

All I could wish in that tiny place. Like an oyster containing a pearl.

We dream and dream of what we want. We can see what we wish to be.

So many times, half-mast flags in our minds. So much we do not set free.

The way one simple action can lead to another and a sequence is put in place.

Out of nowhere, answers fall at our feet without need of pursuit or chase.

And a journey begins that only we can tread, as we make our way down its course.

A step at a time that will get us there. Always driven by a living force.

People presented, at just the right time, to guide us or steer us away.

All designed for our greater good. So that our path is where we will stay.

Imagine we moved from life to life. Gathering more each time we crossed over.

All that learning, over centuries of time, holding the energy of a supernova.

I think of the greats and the heroes passed. Charting and carving new ways.

Focused on the outcome of what their mind sees. Almost counting down the days.

The new giants of the world pushing their limits. Shining like lights in the skies.

Feeling the same as the coward, in the pit of their stomach, but seeing through different eyes.

We see better times where all is well. Just living our perfect life.

It's right there for the taking. It's ours for the making. It could balance on the blade of a knife.

The secret is choice. It's connected to thought. These give our feelings birth.

Every grain of our being. Every ounce of our soul. That's where we can find worth.

The greatest thing we could ever be, are the words of the voice in our head.

We can turn them into action and eliminate distraction. That's when we sew life's thread.

To immerse the soul in more than one goal and drift in a

weightless existence.

Where the small things in life just fall away and one is carried with no resistance.

That is the place to live a life. To feel full by a peace from within.

Like bathing your body in magic waters and being happy inside your skin.

There is always a way to reach a goal. Though the way may never seem clear.

But like a ship setting sail. Facing storms, rain and hail. You will end in a port somewhere near.

Near enough is a test well passed. A percentage beyond compare.

Who is to say what your measure is? What matters is that you are aware.

And to be aware is a gift from life. Only given to those who strive.

It fires in the blood and the belly of those that know that they are alive.

To be alive in a body is a choice that was made. The people. The events and the time.

That you were born at that very moment, so the universe was perfectly aligned.

To embrace your soul from wherever it came and grace it with so much potential.

No conditions therein. Just a life to begin, where results fair inconsequential.

For, trying is succeeding. Effort can be counted. The journey is proof that you travelled.

To look over one's shoulder at a lifetime of memory where all those fruits lay unravelled.

I love the word love. It has so many faces. All those meanings and different levels.

To fly on high through the bluest sky and brush against angels and devils.

Love is in all things. The trees and the winds. Binding everything together.

From the pulse in your heart or a new life to start. Love is every endeavour.

Every feeling you've had. Happy or sad. Love is present to serve all.

In your greatest achievement it will hold your hand and the same if you should ever fall.

It knows no boundaries. It is all your emotions. Any tears of joy or pain.

Whether lacking or abundant. It is never redundant. A long and everlasting chain.

From world to world and life to life. It strides like a lion with pride.

It is a wave of devotion in an endless ocean. That being, the universal tide.

All the wondrous things a mind can create. Great achievements crafted by hands.

Sculptures. Equations. Transformations. In near and distant lands.

The passion and belief of a committed soul can be enough to bring tears to the eyes.

This could trigger our being to do something worth seeing and take everyone by surprise.

So, when our emotions are stirred and we feel unnerved, that is our time to act.

Life's magic is awoken by a feeling unbroken. It is then when love will react.

With all its might it can lift one person, beyond anything they have ever achieved.

That they may reach for the skies and find the same highs as anyone who has ever breathed.

Each person has something to offer the world. They are perfect just as they are.

With all the ingredients to be a great success, which would easily carry them far.

Life is a blank canvas on which to paint. New pictures I will always seek.

These are just a few of my thoughts. Shared with you, my beautiful Monique."

She sat with a stare, as vacant as could be. Assimilating what she just heard.

All he had told her was like a tornado of knowledge, spinning around one little word.

At the eye of the storm where all is calm and everything else acts insane.

This was the feeling she felt all around. Happening outside of her brain.

She looked down at her knees, feeling a bit sick. The expansion of wisdom bore down.

A thousand thoughts trying to squeeze through her mind in which she felt she could easily drown.

Consumed by emotion like never before, she placed both her palms on her face.

Through the gaps in her fingers, she flicked her eyes. Each movement leaving a trace.

She moaned out one breath. Then began to weep. Up became down and vice versa.

If she was in love with his paintings and the person he was, his words served more to convince her.

He stayed where he was. Knowing what he had done. With no effort to comfort or console.

He also knew that in a few short moments she would rejoice at what had been told.

She sat upright, with tears on her cheeks. Her cries slowly turning to laughter.

A blanket of acceptance waved through the air and slowly but surely enwrapped her.

"My god," she said, through the ripples of joy. "What are you doing to my brain?

I understand most of what you say, but now parts of me will not be the same.

You have read some words I have written. There are parallels to what you have said.

We interpret love as individuals through all the information we are fed.

I guess we all see things in different ways. Sharing what we know or are taught.

We then project this out into the world around as the product of a single thought."

They gave each other a knowing look. It seemed like it would never end.

Stillness bounded into the room with the ease of a welcomed friend.

Her stare was fixed. She picked herself up. Then moved to where he was seated.

She opened her legs and climbed onto him. An offering he warmly greeted.

A look of truth. A lover's kiss. Arms reaching round each

other.

Lips to lips. Bosom to chest. New highs for them to discover.
She applied some force. His back met the table. He held her
as close as could be.

The room filled up with a fat swell of sex and a coat of
tranquillity.

Everything was calm. You could hear a pin drop. It was quiet,
like a creeping cat.

A time to let one's senses melt and swirl in a love-drenched
vat.

He straightened his legs and put his heels on the ground. He
brought his ankles together.

She placed the tops of her feet at the base of his shins. To
her, this was sexually clever.

It was all of that and a little bit more. He stiffened between
her legs.

Her lower half made diamond shapes. Up and down without
pausing to rest.

The tie on her robe loosened off, to expose her smooth bare
skin.

Nipples rubbing the silk of her garment. Excitement she
could barely keep in.

It caused a friction that made her writhe. They felt all swollen
and sore.

The more they hurt, the more she turned on. Adding hunger
for so much more.

It was an irritable sensation. Not wanting it to stop. Like
begging to be punished more so.

Until, in the end, she ripped it clean off to focus on the
greater whole.

She brought her arm hard-down on his chest. Cupped his

neck in her hand with force.

Right then, in that moment, she wanted nothing less than frenzied intercourse.

His robe fell open. He was naked beneath. It affected her in a pleasing way.

Actions were the way forward here and there was nothing either needed to say.

Her near-naked body looked an extreme delight. Panties leaving little to hide.

With her other hand she quickly reached down and moved them slightly aside.

Her wetness found his waiting erection. She slid up and down it so slow.

Pushing herself harder to him, so his angst would only grow.

He looked down at himself. He was glistening wet. Made so, by her sex-fuelled enticement.

A little shiver. A churning stomach and a look of pure excitement.

He bit his lip. His top teeth showed. He held a frown of need.

This would be selfish. A part played by each. Hers of wanton, sexual greed.

She slid a bit higher. She was swelling inside. His tip now found its place.

Consuming him wholly in one downward thrust. She had a different look on her face.

A look of disgust. One of scornful contempt. As though punishment were about to be dealt.

He flexed his tenseness between her legs. A sensation she clearly felt.

She blew air out hard. Her cheeks became puffed. She rolled her stomach out.

Guiding him into her pleasure spot. Finding it, she gave a
pout.

She started making circular movements. He felt it on the
smoothness of his tip.

Her eyes lids fell. Her neck twisted sideways. At this point,
she tightened her grip.

He brushed his hands up the sides of her body. His palms
locating her breasts.

His thumb-tips found her swollen nipples. Where they
rotated and gently caressed.

In an inspired flash he was rendered inert. Struck so, by what
she now done.

He almost stopped breathing at the pleasure caused.
Something special had just begun.

Her spine started snaking from top to bottom. She took his
neck in her hands.

This serpentine adoption was highly sexed. Creating tension
and nervous pangs.

She kept her eyes closed. Her top lip curled. She had an
expression of a woman at her height.

She began bucking her pelvis with intentional force. Using
every ounce of her might.

Clasping her hands behind his neck, she brought her face to
his cheek.

These were love strokes, not set to last, as she whispered,
"Do not dare to even speak."

Every time she beat-back, his body jerked forward. He bolted
from his stomach each time.

His hands gripped the chair and he held on tight. He just
took what she did in his stride.

The sound of skin on skin as her buttocks bounced turned

her on like she'd not known before.

She had never forced herself so much on a man. It oozed through her blood to her core.

His expression changed. Her panties had moved. They rubbed him as she shifted up and down.

She moved them again to relieve his pain. At the same time, she removed his frown.

In a perfect move she swung her legs round. With her heels on his buttocks, she dug in.

Finding excellent balance, she clasped his neck. His hands, by his side, were pinned.

Now in full flow, he was where she wanted. Her body temperature was rising.

As a few beads of sweat rolled down her chest, she decided to be more enterprising.

The soles of her feet then lay flat on his chair. She straddled him in a squat position.

There was nothing he could do except take in the view. A slave to her next decision.

Slow, up-and-down movements started leading the way. She looked down between her legs.

Throbbing inside which heightened her ride. Making her feel like she wanted to beg.

The middle of her body started moving around. Her ankles played the pivotal role.

She was climbing inside like the wave of a tide as she reached for her sexual goal.

His arms were numbing, by his side. She opened her legs to release them.

Bringing them round to support her back. He was grateful for this new-found freedom.

He remained submissive. He had little choice. Monique was high on sex.

Bending back her head. Her face was now red. He thought, *What is she going to do next?*

She was way ahead. It was on its way. This would push more than he had ever known.

Moving her cheeks so his legs forced open. She knew this would make him groan.

He placed his soles on the floor. He was bent at the knees. This was exactly what she desired.

She let go of his neck. Pressed her hands on his legs. Only his nerve was what he required.

"Take my wrists," was her clear instruction. He did exactly as he was told.

He felt the weight of her body as she brought her head down. Allowing her back to be rolled.

As she moved away his legs opened wider. His erection made him lean forward.

She freed her hands to reverse-place them on the ground. Done so and not the least bit awkward.

In this crab position, all her ribs showed. Her breasts looked even more tempting.

He placed his face below her chest and his kisses were unrelenting.

Her feet made their way to the backrest of the chair. Finding a place that would assist her to move.

She was penetrated entirely as she slid onto him. The situation would now vastly improve.

He could barely believe the shape she was in. Reaching out, he took her breasts gently.

Nipples to the sky. She was already high. The fulfilment was thrilling and aplenty.

He blew cool air between her legs. It drifted down both thighs.

Quivering at this. A new state of bliss. She let go a few long sighs.

It was happening again. It started stealing her brain. Thoughts quickly becoming sensation.

Flooding down her body like a fall of water. Almost worthy of celebration.

Everything else started to melt from her world. She fought to hold orgasm away.

Ecstasy pursued like a hungry wolf. Determined to consume its prey.

He started driving with intentional force. Her G-spot felt every thrust.

She thought this frantic rate would have her ejaculate, with no one better to let go all her trust.

Her eyes fell closed. She opened her mouth. Her body circled her mind.

His dominant actions were very well placed. His momentum was also well timed.

She was breaking apart. What would ensue? She was touching her soul from afar.

Hot-spots on her skin as she deeply breathed in. Like being kissed by every star.

Always moving toward the feeling as the feeling moved to her.

To be met head-on with the force of a bomb. Done so with no reserve.

Pleasure was stood, knocking on the door. Shouting her to turn the key.

Clawing it away with the ease of dry clay. Demanding she set it free.

She was twisted and cavorting. Losing control. Where would she find middle ground?

Sensing her highs as he held her thighs. Each thrust became more of a pound.

She was over the edge. Hung on a ledge. A pool of orgasm below.

Although she didn't know when, and not sure how, something was going to blow.

He kissed her and touched her. Her body surrendered. Slowly she began to fall apart.

A thousand suns blazed through her soul. It was now time for her to depart.

She was gone from her body. She was out of the room. Her spirit was all that was living.

Cells shattered and regrouped with no chance to recoup. And he just kept on giving.

He was close to orgasm, but she must be first. In his mind, that was how it would be.

She was to tread a path with no turning back that would forever set her free.

Her fingers let go and she started to fall. Like a drip. From a tap. To a bowl.

Every door swung open and snapped off their hinges as energy took a hold.

Like a rocket at a launch pad. Boosters ignited. Fire blasting at the cement chasm.

Lift off was here. Everything was clear. As her mind gave way to orgasm.

It felt like too much. It was almost scary. A rumbling like

galloping horses.

She was a fallen army in the firing line, of all her sexual forces.

In a star-shape position. Not controlling herself. Sex began cracking its whip.

With every lash, her body did thrash. Now, she had no kind of grip.

She did not know breathing. Only feeling. From her feet to both her hands.

A swaying motion like a boat on an ocean. Far away from any lands.

Warm streams emitted from him into her. He could not have foreseen her reaction.

A gushing explosion. Her insides clamped tight. He was forced to a non-optional retraction.

She soaked his body. Her legs slid down. She ended up on the floor.

Uncontrollable jolts in all her limbs. It was something she had not felt before.

She sucked in short breaths. She could not be touched. He was astonished at what took place.

Her eyelids fluttered as her head rolled round. She held a lost look on her face.

She was almost whimpering. Her eyes filled up. She seemed like she was totally possessed.

Large lady twitches. Small bouts of laughter. She lay, pushing out her chest.

She closed her legs and lay on her side. Laughing from the feelings she had.

Bringing her knees close up to her chest, she thought she'd gone sexually mad.

It was by no means over. She couldn't believe it. Her smile was evidence of this.

Orgasmic pleasure still raking inside. It was total feminine bliss.

Her laughter was meant. Its register was low. It was sexy and full of well-being.

Crossing her feet with a feeling so sweet. Connected and, in some way, all-seeing.

Images formed, at dream-like half speed. She had still not come back to earth.

Wriggling around as she lay on the ground. Thoughts filling her with sexual worth.

How could this be? To be so free. Suspended in a world so pure.

Like a drop that hangs on the tip of a leaf. Waiting for a new world to explore.

She clutched her arms and soaked it all up. Thinking, this could not be bettered.

Her sexual senses void of limit. Untarnished and completely unfettered.

He moved to the ground and lay at her back. With one arm he held her to him.

Gently biting the side of her neck. Brushing two fingers under her chin.

It was perfect timing. She warmed to this. His touch made her shiver right through.

Her back pressed his chest. His arm touched her breast. They rejoiced at what they now knew.

"Leon, loving you is effortless. You say and do all the right things.

I love how you treat me with every breath you take, and

everything your warm love brings."

"Monique, you are my lady. I was born for you. I receive more than I could ever give.

When I look in your eyes my heart just flies. That's where I wish to live."

"I want that too. Till the end of time. For you to be my true love forever.

To share. To care. To become more aware. To be joined by love's beautiful tether."

"Monique, we are making it happen. My eyes are for you. You're the only girl for me.

To have my heart stolen in such a way has set my whole soul free.

Channels have opened I never knew existed. It's amazing, the change that's took place.

We have moved to a level beyond belief and done so at such a fast pace.

This, being in love, is the best feeling there is. I see completeness wherever I look.

I hear words in songs that held no meaning before. Now they all marry up."

Still for a moment, taking in what was said. They lay, pondering each other's words.

Hearts in love. Beating together. Both at one with the universe.

They got off the floor and stole a few kisses. She grabbed her robe and put it on.

He picked up his. Did the same. When he looked, he could see she was gone.

A daydream arrived like a train on time. Monique was like a fish on a hook.

Leon turned round. Set himself down and continued to read her book.

Chapter 13

"Easy, Alexander. You are with me again. Sit down before you fall."

"I sat on the grass to let a few moments pass. Still trying to digest it all.

I tried to speak. My throat locked up. I felt I would surely be sick.

Pains in my veins made me clutch at my brains. I thought life was playing a trick.

I took some deep breaths to calm my nerves. I was still a little bit dazed.

The imprints left were like deep cuts. Though, my feelings were completely unfazed.

A taste of earth stayed with me. I sensed it all over my tongue.

It was in my nostrils every time I exhaled. Inhaling, it filled my lungs.

She placed her head on my chest. Her arm on my side. I held her as we lay on the ground.

Her glowing love began to filter through me. It spoke volumes but echoed no sound.

I rolled onto my side and looked in her eyes. My palm touched the smoothness of her face.

This was it. The time was right now. The universe had chosen this place.

I offered my lips to hers. It was a natural thing. Two humans full of love and desire.

Accepting my gesture, she came to me. We were about to unleash all our fire.

Our open mouths joined together. Tongues immediately rotating each other's.

Her touch. Her taste. Her unbelievable grace. Now we would be physical lovers.

As my mind began clearing, my senses returned. I felt feelings higher than ever.

I held her tighter. Caressing her back. My body became light like a feather.

There was not a soul around to disturb the moment. The whole world was busy elsewhere.

Every kiss was electric. Love would be made. Done without a single care.

I peeled her clothes off. She was removing mine. We lay there, naked with the day.

It was something new. Feeling completely on view. We just carried on anyway.

I could feel her yearning. Totally burning. Her fingers pressed deep into me.

No more could she tolerate what she held inside. She was about to set herself free."

"Too much time I have waited for this moment to arrive. I have contained my feelings so long.

My need to make love is now driving my heart. Desire is ever so strong.

I want you, my love. I am yours to have. Let us move to

those reeds by that water."

"As I looked around it was like an oasis was found in a previously unseen quarter."

"Lie down, my love. Let me pleasure your body. I want this to feel like we're in heaven.

Let me kiss your soul. Stroke your skin. We will reach for an unprecedented level."

"I did as she asked. I lay on my back. My cheeks were warm and a little red.

As I met the grass, my whole body relaxed. Like I had slipped onto the sheet of a bed.

She was touching my skin with every fingertip. Sometimes not touching at all.

The sensation was the same, either way. It was exciting like never before.

My naked body was completely alive. Blood pumped like a discharging dam.

She lay upon me and kissed my lips. Stroked my face with both her hands.

I felt deeper in love as every second passed. Harnessed by the greatest force.

A pleasure to accept. Her hands were so adept. She was drawing from the infinite source.

My breathing was quick. It was too exciting. Muscles relaxed, then flexed.

A small breath of laughter escaped from my mouth as I wondered what would be next.

I could not have imagined it in my wildest thoughts. Beyond belief, to say the least.

My vision became blurred. I had to refocus. There was shimmering, like heat being released.

She lay on me and breathed on my neck. A shape began to appear.

Something was born. It was taking form. Initial haziness was starting to clear.

All feeling began to drain from my body. My soul was being physically drawn out.

Charlotte's was too. Something new to view. My senses were full of doubt.

I started to speak. My words were mere whispers. Captured by the very air.

What is this my love? What's going to happen? What are we about to share?

Her lips did not move. I heard her voice. It washed all through my being.

In total wonderment, I was still as a rock. Absorbed by what I was seeing."

"Flow along, with the experience my love. Do not think. Do not act or expect.

Let the questions all go, for the sake of your soul. Later on, we can then reflect."

"I took in what she said. Everything left. We were carried clean into the air.

Our souls faced each other's. Our bodies lay still. All that remained was a loving stare.

More new feelings in this dreamland world. Our souls began to turn and merge.

Slow at the start. I could feel her heart. A sensation I had no wish to purge.

Like twisted candy, colourful and complete, we were becoming one and the same.

The quicker we moved, the more we were soothed. Control

being hard to maintain.

We turned into mist. Now spinning fast. It was only our eyes that remained.

I took all around in as we continued to spin. This cyclone had us contained.

It was tapered and concentric. Perfectly shaped. A living organism all of its own.

Something was building from deep within. It was to let its meaning be shown.

We were being sucked down. Revolutions sped up. Like water escaping a bath.

I felt she knew what was coming. My heart was drumming. All I could hear was her laugh.

We arrived at the eye. Our bodies took form. We were bare and beautiful as we stopped.

Without time to take stock of this briefest pause. A force was then unlocked.

We looked up at the sky. It was blue as could be. Every feeling was crystal clear.

A white circle appeared, right out of nowhere. All was being drawn to here.

An upward draft was going on. A distortion of hearing occurred.

All this energy was being collectively stored. I felt a little unnerved.

Then it was released, in one downward column. As white as fallen snow.

At the speed of light. It gave me a fright. Something was happening below.

We were shot to the sky at a phenomenal rate. Blasting up this tube of mist.

That which was displayed as our exit was made had an extraordinary and welcomed twist.

We burst into lights at unfathomable heights. Screams of euphoria echoed round.

They were filled with excitement. Climactically vibrant, and something much bigger was inbound.

A unification. A higher level of creation. Growing as the seconds passed.

Beyond sexual measure and above simple pleasure. How long could this joyfulness last?

Then the whole world imploded before bursting again. It was a shower of pure magnificence.

Like every orgasm we have ever had was put together in one gigantic experience.

This was a journey. We touched a million stars. Living ecstasy fell like rain.

All the joys that could ever be dreamt sprinkled down and splashed at my brain.

We were taken by something. It laid us flat on our backs. My index fingertip almost met hers.

In the gap between, glowing lights beamed. All with the appearance of small pearls.

Strung together, they started circling our arms. Necks, faces and heads.

They spiralled round our chests and down our bodies like two perfectly uniform threads.

Where they were on me, they were on her too. They now covered our legs and feet.

The gap at our fingers was the same at our toes. The lights joined to make the cycle complete.

A slow buzzing vibration ran through us. When I looked, I

could see her soul glowing.

She looked back at me. I felt ever so free. I also felt my love growing.

The gentle sound of a calm girl's voice released a most beautiful tone.

Like an angel was celebrating a great understanding and letting her feelings be known.

I stretched all my limbs. My spine grew longer. My mouth opened at the feeling created.

Jubilation from such integration. Every cell felt emancipated.

Total flotation. Hanging from nothing. Cool breathing and a mind so clear.

Orgasm present in every second. Cleansed soul without a single smear."

"Alexander, my love. I love you so. I feel like a complete woman, once again.

Every desire has been fully met. It has taken away previous pain.

I am so in love. I could shed tears of joy. I would shout it from the highest mountain.

The infinite source is running up my legs and bursting from my body like a fountain.

Do you feel my feelings? I certainly feel yours. Love has grown and blossomed even more.

This is what I have craved. Right now is what I've wanted. It has so been worth waiting for."

"She turned and rolled right onto me. I embraced her. She had cured all my needs.

One blink of my eyes had me filled with surprise as we lay back amongst the reeds."

"This is nice, my love. Hold me please. Can we lie like this for a while?

My legs touching yours. We'll let the world take a pause. So I can simply smile at your smile."

"I held her gently. Just touching her skin. We were kissing, as lovers do.

A sweet reminder of something I had missed linked with feelings I thought I once knew.

I looked in her eyes and began sharing my mind. A few words from a distant past.

I said, I once thought I was in love. I fooled myself, as it was something not set to last.

Unconditional love could never exist because there was always an underlying fear.

One of giving myself to another person and knowing my love was not dear.

Now love has touched me. I know what it means. No restrictions. No plans. No rules.

The feeling of love is like nothing before. Two hopeless, romantic fools.

Could I love you forever? Of that, there's no doubt. I know I have no need to try.

A thousand reasons to be in love with you from one single look in your eye.

She stroked my face. I closed my eyes. I felt I could fall asleep.

I surrendered to the moment and as I did, calmness washed through with a sweep.

My right arm fell. A cold sensation. My hand became submerged in the lake.

My eyes flicked open. I had a stunned look. I was immediately wide awake.

Water trickled up my arm. I could hear and see it taking place. Reaching my shoulder, it touched my chest. Then splashed at the side of my face.

My mouth filled up. I became completely scared. I thought I would certainly drown.

It poured into my throat and started filling my lungs as it made its way further down.

Convulsions in my stomach made my body jerk. She watched with a lack of care.

One last thrash as my insides ejected. Spewing out all of my air.

Millions of bubbles before my eyes. I started slithering, long and slow.

Like an anaconda at the start of the hunt, I disappeared to the water below.

I remember looking back. Seeing her sitting. Smiling as she admired a small flower.

Snaking side to side, I was becoming Water. I felt an increase of growing power.

I sank further down, to greater depths. Grass swayed. It was catching to the eye.

I ran myself through it. Its gentle touch. A sensation I could not let pass by.

A whirlpool appeared. Its force was strong. I rose and dived in its funnel.

It was black at its centre. I plummeted down. Then sped through a fast-moving tunnel.

I fell off a waterfall in an underground cavern. There were ripples, rivulets and rocks.

Pools carrying water from high points to low. Something akin to old canal locks.

Sprays being formed were refreshing and clear. As high as could possibly be.

I felt every drop on the tip of my tongue. The taste was sweet and clean.

Moving out of the spray, there was a gigantic still lake. The hall opened up even further.

I weaved about at a very slow pace to the sound of low-pitched murmur.

I was not alone. Or, at least, that's how it felt. Nerves penetrated by fear.

Unsettled, I surfaced to try and find safety. Though, that would not help me here.

The stillness was disturbed by an eerie vibration. The water reacted to this.

Millions of ripples in a frenzied dance. Bouncing and making a hiss.

An almighty boom was sent from below. Something rose with swift propulsion.

Climbing fast, after the enormous blast. It was definitely some kind of expulsion.

I could see it nearing. What had done this? I had no means of escape.

I was in the middle of nowhere. At my wits' end. I almost began to pray.

It reached the surface. There was a monstrous explosion. Like a torpedo had hit a ship.

Water burst in every direction. My hold was losing its grip. In an upward shoot, with a whooshing sound, she appeared before my eyes.

I felt so small. She was a hundred feet tall. Now, there was nowhere to hide.

Stood on two white horses, she was very well balanced. A trident hung from her waist.

A green stone on a chain hung round her neck. Between her breasts, it was so well placed.

Her naked body was exquisitely shaped. Her features put me straight in a trance.

She showed me her palms. Looked down at herself. Then gave me a provocative glance.

I was taken in. Under her spell. A look in her eyes had me full of hope.

Her face broke up. I had tunnel vision. It was like looking through a kaleidoscope.

She began crouching down. Then went onto one knee. Her hand came in and cupped me.

Scooping me up, she had a beautiful look. At this point I could see more clearly.

She stood again and brought me close to her mouth. She started blowing into her hand.

As I fell through her fingers, I could feel myself forming. I stood on water as though on land.

We were now eye to eye. My fear subsided. It felt good to be myself, once again.

Although I was far from that in this other world. All became void of strain.

She encouraged me to sit so we could talk. Joining me, she patted my knee.

I crossed my legs tight and sat upright. Then listened to what would be.

"I am the mother and daughter of the element Water. The seas and the rains are mine.

You have a lesson to learn and I am the teacher. This, my

friend, is your time."

"She took my hand and smiled at me. She sat there, nodding her head.

I mirrored her actions. A bit apprehensive. This quickly turned to dread.

She lunged with one hand. It connected to my throat. I struggled to find her reason.

Her skin turned green. She hissed through fanged teeth. Red eyes like that of a demon.

I fought for my life. It was worthless energy. As I struck out it was like trying to hit mist.

With every part of my being I wanted to be free and yet a small part could not resist.

Double vision developed. I was beginning to faint. About to expel my last breath.

She began plunging my head into the water. I guessed my lesson was to get to know death.

I was limp like a rag-doll. Limbs lost their life. I thought my soul would no longer be.

Though I was filled with despair. Yearning for air. The water was setting me free.

My thread on life. A solitary hope. Submerged, I was gulping it down.

Against everything human. I had no other choice. Either live or surely drown.

She took the back of my neck. My head fell forward. I was relieved as she held me aloft.

She stroked up my thigh, my buttocks and back. The touch of her hand was so soft.

Herself, once again, she turned me to her. Still, I was hung in mid-air.

She was beautiful again. I forgot any pain. I reached out and touched her hair.

Drawing me to her, she embraced my body. Confused, I held her too.

Did I laugh or cry? Would I live or die? Things that only she knew."

"Fear not, my dear. I am really a friend, despite what I just put you through.

Now, I have something to expand your mind. It will shake up your senses too."

"With a single hand, she raised me up and threw me into the air.

I looked back down and began to frown as she ran her hand through her hair.

Her manner was cool. Too calm to be true. She moved one hand to her hip.

Looking up at me, then back to her waist, her hand made a very firm grip.

Her trident appeared. A new fate neared. She had lied and lured me in.

I felt so hollow, knowing pain would follow. A short time for it to begin.

It was all so slow. I was floating down. I knew I would not land.

With supreme confidence and a perfect flight, the trident left her hand.

I watched it coming. Three shining blades. The wait after knocking death's door.

The cold steel looked bright. It then spun in flight, so its impact would be felt all the more.

My mind could see it, killing me off. Crashing to my wet,

bloody death.

Her laughing above me. Kicking my corpse. Checking there was no more breath.

Another life taken by this water monster. Then sinking back from whence she came.

Laughing at the outcome of what she had done. Feeling no portion of blame.

Then it burst my gut and ripped through my back. All froze as it peaked in its flight.

It was like being in a snapshot. No feeling or emotion. And yet, something about this felt right.

I had a warm feeling. Was I already dead? Had I crossed over or, in life, somehow moved?

Whatever was happening was bliss to be part of and all my feelings improved."

"I promised you a lesson and this is it. You will remember it for all your years.

When you live in dreams, nothing's what it seems. Whether happy or facing your fears.

To you I was a demon. A monster. An enemy. Hate and fear blinding your path.

I am only a guide to help you see clearly. I offer love and no form of wrath.

In this world, you must read the signs. Let all the negatives dissolve.

Carry love in your heart. Seek only good and you'll always find resolve.

The road is clear. It always is. It's the one place that is eternally true.

Always look for the good in all parts of life and the path will unfold for you."

"She reached down quick and grasped at the water. Then threw it in my direction.

The scene carried on. The trident fell. Taking with it, a part of my mid-section.

I curled in a ball and thought of pain for a second. Then realised there was none to receive.

What happened next was beyond the mind's eye. Almost too much for me to believe.

I burst into ten million droplets. Far and wide. Then fell straight like summer rains.

Landing all over her. She felt so good. I ran through the core of her veins.

I dripped off her fingers. Rolled over her breasts. Slid down her legs to her feet.

This aquatic angel was the force of love. Beautiful and so complete.

I was thankful to her. I could feel it in my heart. She gave so much in a short space of time.

Right in that moment, all stopped again. The whole scene then began to rewind.

It was a heavy drag. My body felt stretched. The strangest sensation I had felt.

Trying to grab anything that would slow me down. What hand would I now be dealt?

My feet felt the earth. My reaction was to stand. I did this though I was heavy as lead.

I gurgled as I spewed out a stomach of water. Then drew air like I was back from the dead."

"Alexander, you're back. That was quick. It seems like you have not been away."

"Charlotte was sat there. Still observing the flower. I wanted to hear what she had to say.

Wading out the water, I collapsed in a heap. Residues still welling from within.

This quickly dispersed now I was no longer immersed. Composed, I waited for her to begin."

"It is gathering, my love. I know you can feel it. Your mind is close to being free.

Come here. Let me hold you. I will warm your skin. Just lay and listen to me.

You can see things now that others cannot. Belief will show you the way.

You have all you will need at any one time or in any one, single day.

What you think in your mind and feel in your heart can exist in no time at all.

Any form of resistance will dissolve in an instance and all defences shall fall.

Others will look to you to show them the way. There are few like you that live.

It is the same in all places. Covering creed and all races. Like them, your duty is to give.

Remember the ebony man and his beautiful looks. His smile. His warmth. His aura.

You, like him, have been blessed with similar charms bestowed on the beautiful Pandora.

Becoming these elements is like opening her box. As though all heaven and hell could not cope.

And at the bottom of her box, almost escaping notice, the ever-beating heart of hope."

"She paused for a time. Then looked to the sky. My gaze became focused elsewhere.

The wheels stopped turning as life held its breath. What I saw commanded my stare.

A red-berry bush, that I had not seen, seemed to grow in brightness and vigour.

Something was happening beyond my control. It was then, life pulled another trigger.

A grey bird flew in and rested on a branch. It just sat there, simply being.

Then it turned to one side. My mouth opened wide. I could not believe what I was seeing.

It revealed its white front. Feathers stood proud. A picture of nature's purity.

One single berry covered part of its white tail as it sat, so full of surety.

Then and there I understood creation. Nothing ever convinced me more.

Representing the feather, I had earlier imagined. With the red dot I had tried to ignore.

Floods of thoughts of all I could dream, lined in my mind side by side.

Like thousands of tulips on summer breezes. Each one embracing the ride.

The infinite source was now obvious to me. This process of making things appear.

I could see that it would endlessly provide, as long as my requests were clear."

"Now you see the signs, my love. You have just turned a key in a door.

You make life happen. You create outcomes. You are capable of so much more.

Our journeys through times are to expand our minds. To

evolve our love and trust.

To where physical being no longer has meaning and all we are turns to dust.

Where we slip away to enjoy every day. Drifting on the good that we are.

Pushed ever-further, in levels of love, as we pass from star to star.

This you will know with the more you grow as love is the only force.

Put everything in with whatever you begin and yours will be a worthy cause.

There is a magic in life, and it is in your palm. To be held up like a beacon of light.

A living embodiment of all that is good. Something real and something right.

So that you are the example for all to observe. And your message is truly heard.

Do you see all the people, gathered around you? Hanging on every word.

I know you can. It's a flash of your future. Images of things, yet, to be seen.

Like a true king, brushing shoulders with subjects. Now there is the dream to be dreamed.

As a saint among sinners who falls to his knees. Then lifting them to where he can see.

So then too, you will find that which is true. In doing so, you will set them free."

"I sat up and faced her. I was so in love. I stroked her arm with my hand.

We both stood up and started walking through this amazing, beautiful land.

The path led up to a forest. Beautifully green. Smoke rose through leaves from within.

I looked at Charlotte. She seemed unconcerned. So we began to make our way in.

It was like another world. As though stepping through a portal. I stopped, to simply stare.

The surrounding sounds and the amplified scents were as welcome as a breath of fresh air.

Deeper in, she put her hand on my chest. I stopped as she went down on one knee.

After sifting about, she plucked something out. Then turned and offered it to me.

It was some kind of plant from the foot of a tree. She put some in her mouth and began chewing.

Accepting it from her, I did the same. Though, I was not quite sure what we were doing.

It had an earthy taste and a pleasing texture. Then the juice it gave off was sweet.

As I swallowed it all, I thought I would fall. I felt warmth on the soles of my feet.

It rose through my body to the top of my head. I closed my eyes and blew out.

When I opened them again it had affected my brain. My perception had been moved about.

Colours were brighter. I felt lighter. I took some deep breaths to calm down.

Despite feeling sickly, I settled quite quickly. Though, my mind was spinning around.

I could now smell smoke. It was not far away. We headed in its direction.

As we were nearing, we saw a circular clearing and somehow,

I felt a connection.

There was a huge fire blazing inside a ring of rocks. We stepped close to feel the heat.

A face appeared from within the flames. Now Fire and I would meet.

His face was friendly and full of compassion. He nodded but no words were spoken.

Being a piece of a jigsaw, I had yet to complete. Thus, making a chain unbroken.

Was it the plant I had eaten? Were my senses now beaten? Could I really see someone there?

As I doubted my eyes, I was taken by surprise. Charlotte pushed me into the flare.

The fire had no bottom. The floor was not there. This was not a comfortable calling.

I was yelling and screaming with frantic feeling. I was falling. Falling. Falling.

Surrounded by flames. My skin burnt to dust. It was free-fall down the deepest hole.

I let a feeling start, deep in my heart. One of maintaining a sense of control.

My eyes glowed red. There were flames everywhere. This tunnel of fire was alive.

Faces whizzed by. None catching my eye. All I wanted was to dive.

It was far too wide for me to touch the side. I did not attempt to try.

I fell for the hell of it. Bent on the experience. Even if my soul were to fry.

Something occurred beyond what I knew. Or even, outside what I could grasp.

Was this a lesson of infinity that I could not measure?
Nausea, now making me gasp.

As quick as a flash I hit the ground. Down on one knee.
Head bowed.

Not a sound all around as I began to look up. Even my
breathing seemed loud.

The floor was black. The surrounding, soft red. It made for a
strange appearance.

I stood up to walk. Just looking around, with a feeling I had
been granted clearance.

As I made my way, I was getting nowhere. All the while,
everything felt hot.

I looked left and right. Paranoid sight. I felt I was walking on
the spot.

All of a sudden, I hit an invisible wall. Bouncing back, my
eyes opened wide.

A feeling of shock, as though being stopped by a rock. Then
everything multiplied.

Lights. Flares. Rockets and bombs. Explosions,
insurmountable and astounding.

I was in a crazed world. Fiery and fierce. Every sound in my
ears was rebounding.

I tried to run. I kept hitting the wall. It was in every direction
I turned.

I laughed at my attempts. There seemed no point, as every
effort was spurned.

A voice came through to calm my unrest. Surely that of the
face I had seen?"

"Stop trying to control the things around you. Yield to the
flow of my dream.

You are here now, and you cannot change it. So relax and I

will let you go."

"I did as he said, and he stuck to his word. Now, what was here for me to know?

A glow appeared in the distance. Quickly, it grew large and drew near.

My ears became full with a familiar sound. Horse hooves were all I could hear.

It was entirely of fire. Majestic movements. Truly, a king amongst its own.

This horse pulled a chariot and I was its passenger. As I boarded, I felt I had grown.

I took up the reins. It was scraping one hoof. Anxious for me to let it loose.

I flexed my arms. It ran for its life, like a hung man freed from a noose.

Holding on tight, I adjusted my stance. One foot forward with my trailing leg planted.

I turned to flames. My body on fire. With a feeling all my wishes had been granted.

All the while, I kept raising my arms. They crashed down like waves on a shore.

The more I did, the faster we went. Then we exploded into a fireball.

I screamed with fury. It was my loudest sound. Fire expelled from my mouth.

Like a comet through space, with a mile-long trace and I just continued to shout.

Ahead was a tunnel. It was for us to enter. Here, we were set right on course.

I stood up straight and pulled on the reins, to slow my flaming horse.

Now at a trot, we entered in. It was black and a warm wind blew.

I heard a roaring crowd. Thousands strong. I couldn't wait for us to get through.

My heart started to beat for what I was about to meet. My horse became uneasy in its demeanour.

A coliseum presented itself. We had now entered a competitive arena.

The cheering peaked. It was a thunderous sound. I looked down to see gladiatorial attire.

I could see no faces as I looked around. Just a free-standing stadium of fire.

Thinking a race must take place, I made my way to the track. I stopped at the starting line.

Three others there. Mere shadows just now. It seemed I had arrived right on time.

I readied myself. Awaiting the start. What the hell was this all about?

Whatever was to come from this surreal situation, I was close to finding out.

I turned to my left. The shadows grew brighter. I stood, open-mouthed, in shock.

The girl from Air. The water goddess. An Earth being made entirely of rock.

They all looked at me. I nodded at them. I was ready for the starting call.

In my heart and stomach a fire was burning. I was going to beat them all.

A woman appeared. She was holding a whip. She began circling it round and round.

When this cracked once, the race was on. We were poised as

we waited for its sound.

She lashed it out and we were off. My horse was possessed and ran fast.

Four circuits passed and we were all neck and neck. How long would this frantic race last?

On the fifth we slowed down. Ceasing to compete. Something sensed beyond the home straight.

As we came round the corner a bright light shone. Stood before it was a golden gate.

The horses stopped. It was a perfect line. Heads bowed, as each breathed from their nose.

The arena fell quiet but only for a moment. An almighty roar then rose.

We all raised our arms and lashed on the reins. The horses began to run.

The gate swung open. We were the glorious, as we burst into a burning sun.

Chapter 14

"My god, Monique. These written words speak. They inspire from a place deep down.

The main character here is slowly losing his fear. Upon his head, will there rest a crown?

What will he do? What will he become? I know you will not tell me, so I'll wait.

Though I will say this, my desire to find out makes me feel like a fish chasing bait.

I must go again. To paint the next picture. Your writing has given me a lift.

It is right there in my mind and I must get it out. I need to create the fifth."

She just smiled politely. Not a single word uttered. He knew she accepted his need.

He stood up and left. Not looking back. Focused only on the upcoming deed.

The light flicked on. The door closed over. An easel was wheeled in place.

He picked up a pencil. Closed his eyes. Then opened his mind to her face.

In his distant thoughts, something was there. He left it so it would find its own way.

As though weaving down a winding path, it presented itself clear as day.

Raising a smile, he felt good inside. Through closed eyes he faced a light.

With this done, he would continue his run and it would make for a wonderful sight.

It was a watch on a chain. Hanging in space. The front open, showing a clock on each side.

The time on one was mirrored by the other. To allow the observer the right to decide.

Monique was stood. A foot resting on each piece. A look that was warm and benevolent.

In big bold letters beneath the watch were the words "Time is irrelevant."

There was a line down the middle. This was a mirror. He wondered, what did it mean?

He stopped for a pause and climbed in his mind. It took him to the edge of a dream.

He thought of reflections and the way they worked. Always distorting the real.

Thinking, one can never really see their true face. Even photos were not real.

The most obvious thing that sprung to mind was simple and immovably true.

That if two people stand in front of the same mirror there is a different them and you.

So the left side of this picture would look a little different. Offset and a little bit misty.

He shouted Monique, quickly three times. She entered the room rather briskly.

"Yes, my love. Is everything alright? You gave me quite a scare."

He didn't say a word. He just looked in her eyes, with an almost vacant stare.

He took her hand and led her to the bathroom. A large mirror hung on view.

Standing at her side, brush strokes being outlined. He smiled as now he knew.

He turned away. She watched him leave. The picture was clear in his head.

Back in his room, he made a start. Scraping and scratching with lead.

The left side of the picture was done in one go. A few hours to get it right.

Distorted to look at. A few blinks required as if checking the strength of one's sight.

Now, care would be taken to create the true image. That, which only the world can see.

The onlookers' perspective. Pure beauty captured. The inner self set free.

As the right side unfolded it was beyond belief. So accurate in every way.

When he finished it off, he picked up a cloth to wipe a few dark parts to grey.

Now to paint. To bring it alive. The birth of a soul in full colour.

The same process as before. Left side first. Of the two, this would be the duller.

As he mixed the paints, he studied them close. To make sure they had a faded look.

Again, closing his eyes, waiting for the snapshot. No matter how long this took.

Like the flash of a camera, every half second or so, the

picture stood before all.

Not only could he see it in the front of his mind. He saw it fixed, hanging on a wall.

He dipped his brush into the paint. Touching canvas with so much care.

A deeper force seemed to guide the stroke as though he were not even there.

It was like he was watching another as it built with colour. He barely blinked in an hour.

A mighty hand, adding meaning to his moves. Taken by a higher power.

This was a different world. A place away. Where things are dragged or placed into minds.

So that souls are presented with all things new and they fall on irreversible times.

And permanent change is observed with each second and every breath is a new birth.

As the desire to inspire transcends human life. So, giving a deep sense of worth.

Hours become seconds and days mean nothing. All that counts is the dream.

Propelled to a level not known by most as the soul breaks into the unseen.

And what is the unseen? Where does it live? How does one find such a place?

That chapel in the mind so easy to find, in the corner of a quiet space.

Existing in all. There to be felt. A spot that, for some, requires prostration.

A place to pray for all one wants. It is the soul and imagination.

To fish all day on infinite choice in a catalogue that never ends.

Pages and pages of limitless options with no regard for what one spends.

Wishes granted in the blink of an eye. Abundance grabs your hands and runs.

Like a mutual friend. No need to pretend. You trail by fingers and thumbs.

Representing positive, and negative too. Both available to clutch or let go.

Each needing the other like a passionate lover in order for each to grow.

Where ideas come forth of their own accord and quality decides a high order.

And a person is pushed to the height of their talent. Then stretched across that border.

In that existence they find their best work. Given freely from their will to yield.

Then free will takes over like a roller coaster and expands their magnetic field.

They get what they give. For that is life. But what they are given can exceed their intention.

Pouring back all their love, they are rewarded more by a process of reinvention.

As new ideas just fall like warm rain. Creating the desire to do more.

Only ever as good as their last achievement or anything that went before.

It was coming together, just as he wanted. He felt the picture was splitting him in two.

He could only focus on the one side for now, so creating a

contrasting view.

A few hours went by. He needed a break. He stopped and went to find Monique.

She had plaited her hair and donned a straw hat which made her look very chic.

He said, "Do you fancy a walk? The mood has gone. It's such a lovely day."

"Of course, my love. I am just about ready. I was coming to call you anyway."

They shut the door. Put their shades on. The day was clear and fine.

A handsome couple, holding hands. Just looking for a simple time.

As they walked, they talked about many things. Mostly of the love they shared.

Pondering the future, with no real plan. As what mattered is that they were paired.

"Leon, my love for you means the world to me. Yes, I have a career to pursue.

But for the rest of my life, if I had to choose, I would spend it here with you.

Contentment is a feeling. Not just a word. Being together has brought this to me.

I see the same in you when I look in your eyes and know it's where you want to be.

It is extremely enriching for the both of us. The balance within is so good.

I kiss your lips when you are fast asleep. Just as a lover should.

I touch your face and stroke your hair. I press my skin on you.

There lies contentment and respectful love. A love that will always be true."

Finding a bench and sitting down. For a minute they watched people walking.

Monique turned to Leon, in a sideways position. She just had to keep on talking.

"I never want to be apart from you. In your presence I am my greatest self.

What you give to me is a sense of purpose. You place me on the highest shelf.

I stand tall and proud knowing I have your love and you have mine for evermore.

If the world would want what I feel in me I would gladly open the door.

To fall in love is a blessing indeed. It must be seen to, like the growing of flowers.

Attention paid to the surrounding force. For it to then unlock its powers.

When we make love, I stare deep in your eyes. I hold you as tight as I can.

I find myself dreaming in the middle of it all. Knowing, that you are my man.

And you are a special man. Such a wonderful being. You care for me all the time.

I feel it when you hold me. Never wanting to control me. So full of reason and rhyme.

My heart skips a beat. I am dizzy to my feet. It is love that brings this about.

So, being together. You and I forever. I know we shall never be without."

Silence fell upon them as they looked at each other. She

looped her hands round his neck.

He turned a little so he could hold her waist. Pursing his lips as she gave him a peck.

It was plain and simple like words on a page. Obvious from the slightest glance.

Observing them would make others feel good. So they yearned for such romance.

Endless love in a thousand directions on a map that was not yet created.

Although paths were there for them to share none were now contemplated.

It was all about now. These breathing moments. Beating hearts so calm.

The mirror of love reflecting a feeling as they slumped in its comforting arm.

Not a single thing mattered as they gazed at each other. Only their love stood out.

Smiles here and there below an unfocused stare brought more good feelings about.

"Leon, it's like a permanent honeymoon when we are together. Every day seems so new.

Infinite possibilities of what to feel next. All good and connected to you.

Needing no translation as it sails so smooth. Like a boat without a rudder and no oar.

Hold me my love, as I may burst from your arms. For the lion is about to roar.

God! I could cry with joy. I could hit all my heights. My soul is ready to fly.

I am a woman in love with all of her heart. I will feel this till the day I die.

My handsome man, please take me home. I want to feel what you feel for me.

Let us make love as the sun goes down and you can tell me how things will be."

The walk was slow. She had touched his heart. His smile remained all the way.

To make love now to his beautiful woman would mark the end of a peaceful day.

He removed her hat and unclothed her slowly. His hands felt all over her skin.

Circling her breasts with the most loving touch so she had a warm feeling within.

They both lay down. He gave her a kiss. His hand slid gently along her side.

This would be sweet. Not a moment rushed. Her smile, she could not hide.

He wanted her to feel loved and she wanted that too. He rolled onto his elbows above her.

Feeling his hard love in that special place, she opened her arms to her lover.

He lifted her neck and put his other arm round her. It was tight and he drew her close.

He freed the other to put it on her shoulder as he rubbed her face with his nose.

Little kisses on her cheek, and too on her lips, had her instantly feeling beat.

Warm breath on her neck and the slightest bite. Her head fell back on the sheet.

He placed his head down and moved at the hips. He felt wetness right on his tip.

A forward movement. Her love opened a little. Allowing a

slow, short slip.

She moaned at this presence. The sensation was exciting. She wanted it all right away.

Using her heels, she tried to make him go further. Even pushing herself up a small way.

He retracted slightly but remained inside her. She was aching to be penetrated deeply.

Setting a slow pace to make her heart race. He would not give this moment up cheaply.

Pivoting at her middle, her sex was building. She felt him rubbing, just inside.

He pushed a little. Slightly deeper. This was only the beginning of the ride.

It was now from the pelvis. His motion was slow. She felt every single push.

Hardly believing the pleasure she was feeling. Understanding his need not to rush.

He kept it slow. Sturdier though. He still held her close to his chest.

Deeper and deeper, he found his way in. To the sound of her quickening breaths.

Like a ticking clock. It was perfect rhythm. He sensed she was starting to go.

Offering all he had with harder, full thrusts. She had a stirring feeling below.

He maintained the same pace. Full and long. Lifting his head, he looked in her eyes.

He rose on his toes. They were nose to nose. Now, he was in full stride.

Between her legs she started jerking. He pushed himself in, one last time.

He was not ready, but she certainly was. That would do him, just fine.

His body was rigid. His elbows sunk deep. Now it was all about Monique.

Selfless love for his adorable woman as he kissed her once on the cheek.

Her midriff movements had her slide on and off. He left it under her control.

He could feel her legs twinging. She moved quick, then slow. Making her orgasm whole.

In the end, she stopped and rested her body. Though she was still in a higher state.

He started again in the very same way. Not allowing her to lower her heart rate.

For the first few strokes she was extremely sensitive. A few "Woos" to get her through.

The bridge was crossed quickly. She had no choice. He knew what he was trying to do.

All out, this time. No slow movements now. She held tight, unlike before.

Her legs wrapped round. She made no sound. He was going to open a new door.

She started slipping away. She was beginning to dream. Unsure of where she was going.

As she closed her eye, she felt she could fly. Thrilled by the sense of not knowing.

It happened fast and it was set to last. Landing first between her thighs.

It filled her stomach. Reached her chest. She dug her fingers into her eyes.

He shook his body. It travelled into her. The vibration,

shaking her right through.

Vigorously hitting the spot each time, she felt like she was splitting in two.

Stopping once more. He had opened the door. Now he would just wait and see.

This was far more powerful, being back to back. Then he could focus on orgasm three.

This was dynamite to her. Shocking, at the least. She asked him to not move at all.

She just lay still but not from free will as the orgasms came all the more.

Shaking with pleasure. Goosebumps all over. Her toes bent at ninety degrees.

If she was stood up now, she would have no chance and simply collapse at the knees.

She opened her eyes and had no sight. But there was something for her to observe.

Thousands of bubbles with a spark in each one started bursting with no reserve.

Still it continued as she blinked her eyes. In the end, she just closed them again.

Surrendering to the orgasms and all that they brought. Loving it, without a scrap of shame.

With no idea of what was happening to her, he was sure she had found a new place.

That's what he thought as her body was taught. It was written all over her face.

Things were slowing up. She was coming down. As she opened her eyes she could see.

Eyeballs like lead when she moved her head. She thought, *How could this possibly be?*

His body ached. He had to move. With his knees he began parting her thighs.

He got up on his hands as he brought his legs round. The relief had him release a few sighs.

Beginning to withdraw, he knew he had more. She did not want to let him go.

Knowing she was high on what had just passed by, his naughty side started to grow.

He sat flat on his shins. Her legs were wide. His forearms brushed behind her knees.

In very small steps, calves slid up biceps. Now he would further aim to please.

Her insteps came up and found his neck. He was clasped in a peculiar way.

The soft skin on her feet was soothingly sweet. This, he could do all day.

He turned his attention to what was in his mind. His arms became straight and tense.

Her rounded cheeks looked like a peach. Now he would recommence.

He started moving. A bobbing motion. Her knees naturally came to meet.

An aroused smile formed. She felt very sexy. His movements became more of a beat.

With a little applied strength, he pushed her legs with his chest. This opened the perfect door.

A calculated movement. To bring an improvement. Now, he would give something more.

On his knees, his angle changed. She felt it and it was right on the path.

Feeling the ridge of his tip, deep inside. At the end of each breath was a laugh.

Taking her by surprise, he quickly changed. Done so, to completely fool her.

When his thrusts went in, he had a grin. Moving as though doing hula.

He was going to find, a way to blow her mind. His erection was rolling around.

Moving at right angles and left angles too. Now, something special had been found.

He was right on her spot. It was driving her wild. Her climax was drawing near.

Coming closer with every push, as she uttered, "Legs, my dear."

He lifted his arms and replaced his palms, so she was free to find her favoured position.

This was a man showing love for his woman. Selfless, before his penultimate addition.

One more thing for him to bring before sharing the moment together.

Placing a wet thumb between her legs, he knew what he had done was clever.

"I'm going to go," as she gripped the sheet. She had never been so ready.

In stimulating her, his thumb was a blur. Now she became very unsteady.

He quickly lay forward on his elbows again. So to give whatever he had left.

Beating his pelvis as fast as he could. He was also close to the edge.

Grabbing her again, for the experience to peak. Their bodies both entered that place.

Where all that matters is what's to come as you look at your lovers' face.

"Oh God," she cried. "Right now," he replied. Pushing in with the final thrust.

Three bursts from his erection. She felt the warmth. It was full of love and lust.

Tensing her stomach, she was in a beautiful world. Her legs fell flat on the bed.

Her arms lay too as orgasm ripped through. Blood rushed straight to her head.

Sweat from his face rolled off his nose and chin. Droplets landed on her breasts.

Her skin was so sensitive that she felt each one. Made obvious by her broken breaths.

He put his tongue on her chest. Then moved to the left. Circling her nipple, slow.

Just for his lover, he moved across to the other. When he was done, he began to blow.

The cool air made her shoulders tense. A whimper was sent from within.

Her beautiful body quivered away. That was a joy for him.

She grabbed a pillow and wrapped it round her ears. Right now, she could take no more.

Rolling over in complete exhaustion, his energy was on the ground floor.

From inside her skin, all was a spin. Making love was always a dream.

The smile on her face said it all. She was the cat that got the cream.

He lay on his side and closed his eyes. A chance for her to reflect on life.

She looked at his face as he lay there still, with thoughts of being his wife.

A couple forever, with lasting love. An ember to never fade. A moving picture of two lives shared in the place where dreams are made.

Clinking glasses at candlelit tables. In locations remote and romantic.

Seeing ruins and relics of Egyptian cities. Exploring islands of the South Atlantic.

Swinging in hammocks, whilst eating fresh fruits. Melon, mango and pear.

Lying on loungers under poolside umbrellas without so much as a single care.

To view the beauty of life. A man and his wife. Stood, watching the glorious sun rise.

Long days in love. Memories to make. Then embrace beneath moonlit skies.

She touched his shoulder. His eyes flicked open. He gave her a closed-mouth smile.

The smooth skin on her leg was met by his hand though the rest of his body was immobile.

She turned her back to him and nestled in. He needed a short time to rest.

Bringing up his arm, he drew her in close and stroked his hand on her chest.

She felt so full as she lay in his arm. Special, like a woman should feel.

Wanting for nothing because she is deeply loved. A thing that could not be more real.

She absorbed it all with her man at her back. A piece of paradise, all of her own.

Sweat on her skin where she made contact with him. As she moved, she made a groan.

Her spine became straight. A tingle was present. It was felt, right through her soul.

Gently, with his nails, he was scraping her neck. She was completely under his control.

Higher, he moved. Into her hair. A small spasm as her head moved to the side.

Smiling as he continued. Down he went. She pushed her breasts out from either side.

She rolled towards him. Her nipples were hard. They were perfect for him to see.

He reached the small of her back. She felt his hard love and fantasised of what would be.

The joy of love could have her weep. She clasped his arm and held tight.

Belonging to something and someone so caring. She was falling in love with this night.

Pictures in her mind, of greater things, played out as though life were giving birth.

Rolling mountains, kissed by the sun, making her feel she was part of Earth.

Not words or just thoughts, but total feelings. Where messages are sent to find.

With no impurities. Like drops from heaven. A creation cast from the mind.

A path with no ending on another plane. Winding into the distance, from sight.

On tracks never trodden by human feet. The place of eternal delight.

Down hills into valleys like tumbling winds. Touching every

tree and leaf.

Where every atom is super-charged with an unwavering feeling of belief.

She believed in love. She always had. Though she never thought it would be as good as this.

He rolled away. She rolled to him. Time to find some more bliss.

She started smothering him with the warmth of her skin. Her chest pressed on his back.

Lifting her leg to wrap around his. Her arm following a similar track.

His breathing grew heavy. He was drifting to sleep. She rested her face on his skin.

Listening to the sound of him slipping away and also the tide coming in.

The sun was done but she was not. She held on to her sleeping lover.

Falling backwards, to the depths of her mind, as she gently pulled over the cover.

A crack in the curtains allowed her a view. Stars, in a clear night sky.

Placed there for lovers. Some brighter than others. One of them catching her eye.

It took her thoughts to deep inside. The muscles in her face relaxed.

She let it happen and accepted the flow, no matter how much time elapsed.

Eyes now blank. Her mouth was open. Breathing could not be heard.

Heart beat slowing. Temperature dropping. Reality being transferred.

She had quickly crossed over to the unseen place where power and magic reside.

And secrets are revealed to willing heroes, so they take charge of life's wonderful ride.

Her imagination was taking flight. Enhanced by darkness all around.

A perfect setting for a soul to swim as her ears became mute to sound.

Before her eyes, shapes were forming. Undefined with no real direction.

Like traces from sparklers. Gold, magic dust. Releasing waves of introspection.

Her senses at large. Uncertainty in charge. She delved inside her soul.

Although sleep was close by, she blinked her eye. So to focus on the unseen goal.

To her it was clear. There was a message here and she would stay to the bitter end.

Something was gathering, inside and out. It was warming like the love of a friend.

Her glazed eyes were wide. She felt excitement. Like a child who is awake and dreaming.

Where all things are fun, real and fantastic. With no care for a specific meaning.

In a sweeping flow she could only let go as a creation came to the fore.

Stars and streams. Things of dreams. From the ceiling down to the floor.

Like a magnificent fountain, right on view, expelling some wonderful things.

She saw carousels and wishing wells. Bells and golden rings.

Bursting out, like a firework peaking, from every corner of her mind.

Mumbling at one point, without even knowing, as clarity was being outlined.

A tune, in her ears, began to play. It echoed and its sound was eerie.

Like an untutored child plinking a piano. Comforting, despite sounding dreary.

Everything moved closer. Her dead jaw dropped. She was becoming part of the scene.

Past her unflinching eye, a lark flew by as she balanced between reality and a dream.

She heard her pulse. It was beating slowly. Something was about to start.

As it showed itself, she could only smile. She fell asleep to the sight of a gold heart.

Chapter 15

Leon woke first and gazed at her sleeping. He started removing the cover.

Her naked body was soon exposed. Now, to wake up his lover.

He sat himself up. Walked round the bed. Smiling, as he knew what would be.

Touching her skin as he took it all in. He gently pushed forward her knee.

Her modesty exposed. She was still fast asleep. He stroked her leg to the top.

Lying behind her. Head away from the pillows. Though he wanted to, he could not stop.

He parted her cheeks, which opened her love. Her scent was sweet and inviting.

Like a drug to an addict, he just had to continue. It was sexual and highly exciting.

He took a moment as his tongue wet his lips. Placing his nose just inside her.

He kissed a few times. She became moist. Further strengthening the aroma.

She breathed in deeper. Not yet stirring. He froze. His heartbeat sped.

He gave it a moment. Let out his air. Then transferred the thoughts in his head.

His tongue was wet. Thin at the end. Pushing in, made his face squint.

Her taste was strong. He was erect in seconds. His eyes had a hint of a glint.

Parting her further, he changed his stroke. Delicate, on her softest skin.

Not wanting her to wake. At least, not just for now. As her juice wet his lips and chin.

In her deepest dream she was on a white bed. Still mist sat at all sides.

Soft as silk and reaching for miles. This was a place in the skies.

Like a vestal virgin waiting to be taken. To become a woman in a fully renewed world.

Only pillows for company but wanting her man. Leaving behind the untouched girl.

Columns stood, in a circular boundary. A point where only one more were permitted.

Crossing this was a devotion to love and that person would spend a lifetime committed.

And her love appeared in all his glory. As naked as the day he was born.

She gazed upon him from over her shoulder. Admiring his perfect form.

Her hand reached out. He dropped to one knee. Taking and kissing her arm.

Turning it over as his fingers caressed. She felt his warm breath on her palm.

Standing again, he placed one knee on the bed. She cupped

him and rubbed with affection.

She felt a strong sensation between her legs as she brought him to a full erection.

Like a warrior who had battled for the heart of a woman.

Now, he was claiming his prize.

From deep in her heart she knew what she wanted. It showed in her smouldering eyes.

She touched her breasts and opened her legs. Commanding a swift reaction.

In the briefest moment he was lying upon her. Intent on her satisfaction.

No pause required. She offered her love. It glistened from the sexual highs.

Entering her slowly, she felt every step as she clasped him with both her thighs.

She felt herself falling. She woke with a shock. Leon held her close to him.

He was deep inside her. She was highly turned on. What a way for her day to begin.

She moaned with pleasure into his ear. He was in full stride, breathing deep.

Crossing her feet behind his back, knowing he was hers to keep.

She would make this for him. Just for her love. She embraced him and spoke as he rode.

"I love you, my love. I only want your joy. When you are ready just let it explode."

This affected his mind in a wonderful way. He moved at a phenomenal rate.

He could not hold it. He was too overjoyed. He was going to ejaculate.

Then, on his palms with straightened arms, he looked down at her beautiful face.

Spine bent back. Not one muscle slack. It was a picture of sexual grace.

He bowed his head and closed his eyes. She jolted her pelvis for him.

He barely moved. He had no need, as she guided him out then in.

Her heels on his legs. Hands on his ribs. She was ready to orgasm too.

His groaning now louder with every breath. Just about ready to break through.

At the point of unleash, his head flipped back. His warmth shot deep in her love.

She twitched fiercely. Her upper legs shook. He lowered himself down from above.

He held her close. As still as a rock. Knowing she was in that orgasmic place.

Her stuttering breaths. Her stiff-nipple breasts and that distraught look on her face.

Like pleasurable pain one can barely contain. As sex has pushed you with all its force.

You feel alive as your body says yes because you have just had inspired intercourse.

He remained inside her. Just holding on. She held him in much the same way.

Passion was present. They began to kiss. All part of a gentle sway.

"You're so selfless Monique. Such kindness is a gift. I feel your love for me.

Be sure of my love for it will never fade from now to eternity.

I care not for the past. Its time is done. Forward is where I wish to place my mind.

Doing that is easy enough when I am in love with someone so kind."

His thoughts snapped in two like a dead, rotten branch.

Crushed, by the sole of a shoe.

Through the debris, an unclear spike of knowledge flashed by within a second or two.

A draining feeling shot through his being. Mouth dropped as his eyes drew blank.

Sickness in his stomach. A hard lump in the throat.

Exhaustion of all fuel from the tank.

Her eyes were closed. He rolled away. She knew nothing. He would keep it this way.

A cloud of grey quickly turned black. There was nothing he could think of to say.

Something was wrong. Unable to pin it, he sat up and put his feet on the floor.

Sluggish movements as he stood himself up. Behind him, he closed the door.

Pouring coffee he'd made, he could not shake it off. He stepped out to the warmth of the day.

The love in the world had found him lost. Feeling someone or something would pay.

Sat in a chair, palm over his ear, his back arched as his shoulders dropped down.

A negative flood coursed through his blood. His insides were spinning round.

He sipped away and looked at the day. No interest in the surroundings at all.

Monique appeared. Coffee in hand. With a look that said it all.

"Leon, my love, I feel so good. Look at this glorious
morning."

In a flash of a second she could see he was down and decided
to carry on talking.

"You seem troubled my love. Share it with me. We can work
anything out together.

Let it all go. Let your feelings show. So, once again, you can
feel light as a feather."

"Monique, I do not even know what has shaken me so. A
cloud found me and rained down heavy."

"So cast it away and join the day. Life is rich and you are wise
and heady.

You're a wonderful man so why give a damn? Just smile and
I'll do the same.

I swear I will drag you for as long as it takes to put your mind
into a different frame."

Lifting his head, he took a deep breath. An attempt to get a
hold on esteem.

Thinking of things to be thankful for. To thread together in a
continuous stream.

The chain started building and weaving a way. As though a
magic wand was being waved.

A sense of relief began to grow, which give him a feeling like
he had just been saved.

Then a splinter of doubt began to shout. A lone piece that
would not rest.

Shaking his head to distract this thought, he knew it was just
a test.

The day was bright. He looked at his love. She had done it
without even trying.

A few sharp words had straightened him out. So easy and so

gratifying.

Another coffee and they were ready to move. A trip down the coast was decided upon.

Leon drove the car round. Flipped the roof down and gave her a look of assured aplomb.

A two-seater soft-top he had never mentioned. She smiled with joy in her eyes.

He kinked his top lip. Winked at her once. Then coolly said the word, "Surprise."

She jumped on the spot like an excited child. Clapping hands, as if to say yes.

Then taking a place in the passenger seat, she thought, *This man knows how to impress.*

They drove for miles without saying a word. The views were enough on their own.

Bustling bays. Villas on hillsides. Some wonderful and colourful homes.

It was nearing midday. The sun was hot. They pulled over to get something to eat.

Finding a small café that had outside seating, with large umbrellas to escape the heat.

Balsamic vinegar with olive oil and a basket of freshly baked bread.

A jug of iced water and a couple of glasses. Cold flannels for the face and head.

Then they both had bruschetta, with all the trimmings. A delightful, local dish.

To finish it off they had a third course of the finest, freshly smoked fish.

Simple pleasures from such short measures. They hardly took their eyes off each other.

Such is the way when two are this way. Life just revolves round your lover.

The cheque was paid. A tip was made. "Arrivederci," then back to the car.

She was more than pleased as he threw her the keys. He'd already driven quite far.

The sun on his skin made him feel like lead. Eyelids dropped as sleep set in.

His head fell to one side from the comfort of the ride. Time for dreams to begin.

She shot him a glance. Then back to the road. A smile spread across her face.

Some time for her, to think about love. To put herself in a perfect place.

Her hair blew in the wind like golden silk. Sunglasses keeping sharp edges soft.

Thoughts rolling out like a breeze over grass as she sensed the odd coastal waft.

She thought about sex. Now, her favourite thing. She had never had so much in her life.

The delicate touches. Passionate kisses. One day to become a wife.

The pre-orgasm build-ups that come in stages. The secrecy of what would be next.

Those points where her body was so overcome. The feeling of being highly sexed.

Unafraid of her feelings and, less, her thoughts. She continued to bring fantasies about.

She imagined them naked. Him on his back, as she took all of him in her mouth.

Scraping his chest as she straddled his legs. Moving her head very quick.

Pulling back his skin. Exposing him. Then offering a loving, full-length lick.

Her warm, wet mouth sucking his tip, made her squirm and her pelvis roll.

Pleasure was growing. Boundaries not showing. Dispensing of all control.

She was wildly in love and she was going to show it. Sex unsheathed its sword.

Plunging it deep and straight up her spine like a mighty overlord.

She clasped her breasts and pushed them up. They were either side of his erection.

Still with him, just in her mouth. A swift, up and down direction.

She carried this on. No way would she stop. Almost snarling. A slave to sex.

Faster she went. Every action well meant. Sweat gathering between her breasts.

She needed it in her. She could wait no more. She felt she was going to explode.

In one quick slide she moved herself up. Then reigned down before he could unload.

It felt high in her stomach. She loved every bit. A shock to take it all in one go.

She bucked him hard with forceful intent. All done whilst clenching his throat.

Her eyelids fluttering as she began muttering. Comments that she was about to peak.

In that moment the fantasy expired, just as she was going to speak.

She almost forgot she had been driving. Little care. She found herself in a heightened state.

The gushing emotions were full of sex. Not yet ready to dissipate.

Without hesitation, because she was naughty, she took one hand off the wheel.

She slipped it down between her legs. A moment she had to steal.

Her middle two fingers found her love. She rotated with frantic haste.

She then brought them up and placed them in her mouth. Just to catch a taste.

Looking down at her nipples which were pushing out. She rubbed each one quite fast.

Then back in her panties to carry on. Knowing this was not going to last.

Her love was pouting. She felt like shouting. Juice ran between her cheeks.

Slippery as cream. She was in a dream. Like every woman that peaks.

Faster she went. Swerving a bend. Then ahead was a long, wide straight.

The soft wind blew in all directions. What a time to masturbate.

She bent forward her back. Let out a laugh. It was amazing. She felt so high.

Her reddened face was beginning to perspire, and she had that look in her eye.

It was very powerful. Building fast. Thighs, tightening on her hand.

Her stomach was tingling. Bottom lip quivering. Orgasm

about to land.

Highly dangerous. Just what she wanted. Her foot pressed harder on the gas.

Testing herself. To see if she could ride it. Now for the pleasure blast.

Her eyeballs were rolling. She breathed through her nose. Her body shook hard in the seat.

It roared like a rocket. Sparks in her vision. Exquisite and sexually complete.

Rapid breaths to calm herself down. Still, she was shaking like a leaf.

She knew what she had done was crazy, at best. But what a sense of relief.

Her panties were soaked. Her fingers remained. She rubbed slowly and it felt so good.

Touching her outside spot with every pass. So sensitive as she drew back the hood.

Leon was gone. She was highly turned on. So, deciding to give him a treat.

She rubbed her wet fingers on his lips. Knowing, the taste would be sweet.

His tongue poked through his lips. It was now in his mouth. The scent, drifting up his nose.

Turning her hand over, she moistened his nostrils. From between his legs, a bulge arose.

For her, seeing this was total bliss. She caressed and cupped her breast.

His trousers were no match as she started to scratch. Sex would not let her rest.

She opened his zipper and spread it wide. Moving his shorts, she took hold of him.

Still pliable enough for her to draw it free. She fully pulled back the skin.

Slow, gentle strokes. He became fully stiff. She thought, *Surely he will wake any time.*

She snorted a laugh. She felt like a devil. She knew she was committing a crime.

No one around. A lay by ahead. She slowed down and pulled the car over.

She couldn't believe he was still fast asleep. Caring not, as instinct drove her.

Removing her seatbelt and adjusting her rear. She acquired a favourable position.

Her mouth was on him as her hand slowly worked. This was an inspired decision.

Her heart was pounding because she knew it was wrong. Naughtiness told her it was right.

She thrust her free hand in her panties again. Now it was dynamite.

What thrilled her most and turned her on is that she could be caught at any time.

Carrying on anyway, her fingers plunged deep. Her legs were open wide.

It was now a challenge. He was stiff in her mouth. The mere thought made her dizzy with lust.

Could she carry it through without waking him up? This, to her, was a must.

She applied more care. A steady rhythm. Then, she went firm and slow.

Her mind going crazy with sexual excitement. Hoping he would never know.

Knowing he was flowing set her off again. Struggling, not to grip too tight.

Head bobbing quicker. In her mouth he grew thicker. Her fingers creating delight.

Hearing a snore, she knew she could do it. Lifting up, she now sucked at the tip.

Moving finger and thumb. This would soon be done. At one point she licked her lip.

Bending her fingers inside herself. Flashing over her dimpled G-spot.

Faster, she moved. Trying to hold on in this wild and perilous plot.

Below his erection he was tightening fast. Everything drawn and ready.

Her two hands now worked. Pleasuring them both. Her body becoming unsteady.

His tip swelled in her mouth. This was it. She clung on to the final thread.

One second ticked. His body kicked as she quickly plunged down her head.

A massive burst inside her mouth made her peak at the very same time.

Swallowing slowly as her fingers still moved. Now, it was the perfect crime.

She remained a few seconds. Until it was done. Her body felt more at ease.

Zipping him up. She sat up to look. In herself, she was more than pleased.

The engine still running. A glance in the mirror. She smiled at an approaching car.

It pulled in behind as she sped away. Feeling like an adult movie star.

Now mid-afternoon, she felt he'd slept enough. Wanting him to re-join the day.

She shook his leg and started saying his name, now that she'd had her way.

He woke real slowly. He had slept very deep. Unaware of what had been done to him.

Looking at her, he made a frown. Wondering why she had such a large grin.

"Are you happy Monique? Are you still in love? Will you stay for the rest of your life?"

They both began laughing as he yawned and stretched, saying, "I still want you as my wife."

"I am all of those things and I want the same. Shall we stop somewhere for a drink?"

He said, "Our destination is almost upon us. This place you will like, I think."

The sea looked amazing. A few more miles. The road forked. He pointed the way.

At the end of a lane was a large coffee house, overlooking a beautiful bay.

They found a space. Went inside. Air-con and soft leather seats.

A drenching scent. Familiar and rich. It was that of ground coffee beans.

Large glass panes across the back of the building. Giving spectacular views.

Sea birds of all sizes. Circling and darting. Constantly searching for food.

A tranquil atmosphere. Faint music played. Perfect, against the scene.

The sun, half-high, in a clear blue sky. The sea, as always, pristine.

Ordering coffee which arrived in minutes. They relaxed, giving each other a smile.

Leon reflecting on times gone by and how he had not been here for a while.

There had been no need. Too far to come. A journey he would not make alone.

Apart from his gallery and Amsterdam, recent years had been spent at his home.

She said, "You have been here many times. It shows in your eyes. Like you have just revisited your past."

"I love this place with all my heart. It's funny how fond memories last."

They finished their drinks. He suggested a walk. They left through an exit at the rear.

Taking her hand, he said, "This way, my love. There are steps to the beach over here."

They were really old. Carved from the stone. The railings, having had their day.

Mainly walking side-on as some edges were now gone. They began to make their way.

Far from straight and steep at all times. The gap between them grew.

Now the child again that had been here so often. Leon, ignoring the view.

Monique took a pause to appreciate the place. The sound. The smell. The sight.

Placing her hand on the rough stone face. Sandy yellow against the sun's light.

Looking back for the first time, he had reached the bottom. She had a way to go.

Forgetting the ocean in favour of her. A picture, in his mind,
did grow.

Watching her move. Getting closer. It became clearer with
each step she made.

Looking at him as she got to the bottom. That's when the
whole thing played.

He would remember this moment. Perfect on canvas.
Captured right on time.

Seeing what was happening, she froze for a moment. Before
continuing on with a smile.

Greeted with a kiss and a firm hug to match. Picking her up
at her waist.

He turned her round once, placed her down. He had a look
of youthful chaste.

It was nearly five as he looked at his watch. There were hours
still left in the day.

They started walking. Holding hands. Watching some
children play.

She gave him a look. It was full of love. Desire was set on her
face.

He was not looking. Too busy dreaming. So fond of this
beautiful place.

She said, "Leon, my love. You know what's great. Something
I just need to say.

In this very old world, all that matters is living with you day
to day.

This, right now. Just being with you. Sharing this part of your
past.

We'll come here again. It is now part of our future. Make
memories set to last.

It's like I have forgotten who I was. A brand-new life.

Routines have dissolved to nought.

My body is relaxed. Along with my mind. Opening channels of inspired thought.

I've had this idea. It's been rolling around. Based on a future time.

An erotic story. Explicitly descriptive. I would call it My Wife and I.

Difficult to do but I would give it a go. The male character is where I would place perspective.

Translate the love we make in a fictitious way. So, for us, it would be purely reflective.

It has got me excited in a sexy way. The beauty is that no one would know.

We make love. I turn it to words. Then sit back and watch a story grow."

He gave her a smile whilst nodding his head. Instantly intrigued, wanting more.

Saying, "Can we go home now and make a start? It could begin on the bathroom floor."

They burst out laughing and hugged one another. He tried to kiss her but simply could not.

He let her go. Put his hands on his knees. He was absolutely nailed to the spot.

Crossing her hands, she slumped on his back. His comment was a brilliant retort.

They took a moment. Gathered themselves. Then kissed and embraced once more.

She looked at sea as he stood at her side. Familiar sounds filling her ears.

All she could feel is that she was in love. She wanted it for all her years.

Watching waves, as each one rolled. Thinking, how her life
was so good.

Looking back, to when she was alone. Something new to be
understood.

In earlier times, she thought her life was full. Happy, in the
day-to-day things.

It was now overflowing. Continually growing, with all the joy
that love brings.

She thought, *I could daydream all day. Then write it down. That's all
I've done up to now.*

Such a nice way to carry on. New ideas would find her,
somehow.

It's what she had done. That's who she was. Life had always
provided a way.

Showing courage before. She could do it once more. Sharing
what she had to say.

"Monique, we should move. The tide is coming in. It moves
fast and the steps are our way out."

They turned and walked. Having come quite far. Moving
quickly. Not hanging about.

The sounds grew louder. The waves crashed harder. Rocks
being hit further down.

She grew a little nervous as he grabbed her hand. Thinking, a
person could easily drown.

In the distance, people were moving. Scurrying with towels
and possessions.

Locals who knew the presented dangers of getting caught in
these rapid progressions.

Now it was scary. They were still far away. The sea began
splashing at the steps.

He said, "Run Monique. We have to make it or I swear we

will have regrets."

She threw off her shoes and started to sprint. Panic had her shaking with fear.

He was right on her tail. He'd been here before. Their exit, by no means, near.

The beach was thinning. The wash became greater. Waves now breaking on the wall.

It was like an escape door closing. Sealing everything in. A place where all shall fall.

As fast as they ran, they were not going to make it. She sensed this and was already crying.

Grief overcome her as the oxygen expired. She thought, *This is not a day for dying.*

Survival carried her. She kept ploughing forward. Blinded by the will to live.

The situation had a shock in store. Life had something sinister to give.

Leon's heart sank. He saw it coming. A wave, bigger than any other.

He tried to grab her. Too far away. He screamed, "Monique!! Take cover!!"

A virgin to this. His words made no sense. Too late to collate or digest.

Even if they registered, there was no time to react. She would soon be crowned by the crest.

It barrel-rolled. It looked like a cannon. Cooled air shot through its shaft.

He grabbed at the rocks. It smashed at her body. Then unleashed a mighty downdraft.

Diving in, he reached out an arm. Clutching at anything that was there.

By some divine miracle he did catch something. He yanked her up by her hair.

They only had moments. Not time to waste. She spat out a mouthful and stood.

He started running. Dragging her with him. Before the onslaught of the next tidal flood.

Seeing the white railing, he dug in deeper. Throwing everything at this final try.

Judging the distance, he looked at the tide. They had to make it this time.

The sea dragged back, revealing some sand. The next wave was bigger again.

He reached the foot of the steps and held her tight as the sea unleashed more pain.

Lashing with a force that blew them off their feet. Their backs hit the railing hard.

They were lifted ten steps as the wave backed off. Still, he had hold of her arm.

Her body was limp. Lying unconscious. Blood on the back of her clothes.

As he picked her up, her face was white. More blood now came from her nose.

He put her over his shoulder and started climbing. As fast as his legs would go.

Sprays from the sea as the waves crashed again. His panic now starting to grow.

His lungs felt pain. He didn't care. Safety was the place he sought.

Looking up once, he could see the top. Reaching it was a comforting thought.

He kept saying her name, to no response. He was close to

tears with sadness.

Cursing himself that he had been so naïve. His heart now filling with badness.

Grinding his teeth. A devilish sneer. Rage thundered through every cell.

Carrying his whole world over his shoulder. This was a living hell.

He took the last step and placed her down. He looked round. There was no one about.

The shop had shut. The cars had all gone. The word "help" was all he could shout.

He held the back of her neck. It was covered in blood. He didn't know what to do.

Something kicked in. He pinched her nose. Then opened her mouth and blew.

He pressed hard on her chest. Then on her stomach. A critical point had come.

If she didn't breathe soon, she might never again. This thought made him numb.

She was turning grey. Slipping away. Through his tears he kept on trying.

A fragile frame is all that would remain, as now she was close to dying.

He was on his own. All alone. Swearing out at the wretched seas.

Rocking her body. Holding her close. Life ignored all his pleas.

Stroking her chest. Wiping blood from her face. How could he have been such a fool?

Laying her down as soft as he could. Thinking, *Can life really be this cruel?*

A twitch. A reaction. A stomach contraction. Water spewed

out of her mouth.

The intake of air had a shriek attached. The exhale harboured a shout.

His whole world changed. So had hers. He rubbed her to get her blood pumping.

Her eyes were glazed. Pupils were huge. His heart was literally jumping.

She vomited more water. At least she was breathing. Even though she had a long-lost stare.

Calling her name. Shaking her face, to somehow try and make her aware.

Her soul was floating. Looking down at the scene. She looked dead and that could still be.

She felt like an angel who was moving on. Removed from her body and set free.

It didn't last long. She thought, *Do I have a choice? Is the decision to be left with me?*

If that is the case, then I choose to return. With my love is where I must be.

Like a medical syringe, drawing blood. Her body began to suck back her soul.

A racing feeling grew big and strong. Making her, once again, whole.

She could not have imagined it in any life. A flash of white light and she was alive.

Coughing and screaming. No longer dreaming. Her mind entered overdrive.

It was not her own. She had been adjusted. The trauma had left her displaced.

Wild eyes blinking. All feelings sinking. Everything was being retraced.

Finding no grip on who she was. A character in a horrific tale. Why did he touch her? This disgusting man. She would see him locked up in jail.

She looked in his eyes but did not know him. A stranger in another form.

Where was she, and who was he? She felt like she had just been born.

Born into a world she did not know. A nightmare existence she hated.

She started kicking her legs and scratching his face. Rationale not even debated.

Everything was alien. Where was this place? As she writhed, she was surrounded by dust.

Still dizzy from the experience. Feeling sick. She was more than a little concussed.

How could he comfort her? What could he do? He spoke to try and calm her down.

"Monique, my love. We must get you to hospital. We both just nearly drowned."

Clearly delirious, shaking her head. With every second her blood was getting low.

He was so concerned that he moved towards her. She had sustained a heavy blow.

Rejecting his offer, she moved further back. Showing his palms, he told her to stop.

"Please Monique. Don't move any further. You are so close to a sheer drop.

You must listen to me. You are not yourself. I want to help you. You are heavily bleeding."

At this point in time he went down on his knees. Upset, had him begging and pleading.

Her colour was draining. She began to look weak. Functions beginning to fail.

Blood from her nose entered her mouth. Tacky and sickeningly stale.

She started to whimper. Feeling scared. Her world was a daunting place.

Falling back on her elbows. Crying out loud. Tears now streaked her face.

He begged her again to let him help. Now, he was scared to get near.

One false move and she could hurt herself. This was his deepest fear.

"Monique, stop this madness. Come to me. My love, will you please take my arms?"

Again, he reached out, sensing her doubt. He just held out his palms.

Something in her mind recognised his voice. Though scared, she could see his grief.

Spitting out blood and trying to smile. Here was someone she wanted to believe.

She said, "Stay there. Don't move. I think I know you. Give me a moment to check."

Dropping her head. Feeling sharp pains. She put her hand on the back of her neck.

She closed her eyes. This did not help. Dizzy, more than before.

When she opened them again, he was standing. Raising her fear once more.

"Get back I said. Don't come any closer." Scrambling to get to her feet.

She was a step from the edge of the end of her life. It was

something she could not see.

He froze on the spot. Four paces away. Shaking all over with dread.

If she moved a fraction it would all be over, and she would surely be dead.

Then everything cleared. It all became nice. She knew him as the man in her life.

The earlier daydream, where she had seen herself, now helped her to see through the strife.

"Leon, it's you. Where are we? I don't know this place at all."

"Monique do not move. You have hurt yourself. Be careful you do not fall.

Come to me. Please give me your hand. You need medical attention right now.

You have lost lots of blood. We have to move. We must get to the nearest town."

"I'm fine," she said. "What's the panic?" Her knees wobbled then went completely stiff.

To reset herself she moved her foot back. Stones fell off the edge of the cliff.

Her smile remained. She was going to faint. Seeing her rocking, he lunged.

She fell backwards. Arms at her side. Her feet come unstuck and she plunged.

It was super-slow motion. This was not happening. His fingers made contact with her toe.

His world broke in two. His face bit the dust. With horror, he screamed the word

"Noooooooooooooooo!!!!!!!"

To be continued…

Printed in Great Britain
by Amazon

71153724R00129